Manifestation and the Multiverse

Manifestation and the Multiverse

Your Life Can Change at Any Moment

Moon Li and Jonathan Soul

HOUNDSTOOTH
PRESS

COPYRIGHT © 2025 MOON LI AND JONATHAN SOUL
All rights reserved.

MANIFESTATION AND THE MULTIVERSE
Your Life Can Change at Any Moment

FIRST EDITION

ISBN 978-1-5445-4882-1 *Hardcover*
       978-1-5445-4881-4 *Paperback*
       978-1-5445-4880-7 *Ebook*

Contents

INTRODUCTION 9

PART 1: THE MULTIVERSE
1. YOUR ALTERNATE SELVES 19
2. THE FIERY SELF 23
3. THE BRILLIANT SELF 29
4. THE CALM SELF 35
5. THE CONFIDENT SELF 43
6. THE IMAGINATIVE SELF 51
7. THE FREE-SPIRITED SELF 61
8. THE EXTRAORDINARY SELF 71
9. THE IRRESISTIBLE SELF 85
10. THE POSITIVE SELF 99

PART 2: BARRIERS TO INFLECTION POINTS
11. DOUBT 113
12. THE WRONG PATH 117
13. INSECURITY 123
14. BEING BURNED OUT 127

15. IMPATIENCE 131
16. LACK OF MOTIVATION 135
17. BEATING YOURSELF DOWN.. 139
18. FEAR 143

PART 3: YOUR UNFULFILLED SELVES
19. THE LOST SELF 153
20. THE LONELY SELF 159
21. THE PESSIMISTIC SELF 165
22. THE NUMB SELF.. 171

CONCLUSION 179

Introduction

IMAGINE YOU HAD CHOSEN THE OTHER PATH.

Imagine you had taken the other job. Gone on a date with the other person. Chosen the other major or college. Moved to the other city.

Or imagine even a seemingly slight change. On one fateful day, you took the stairs rather than the elevator. And because you took the stairs, you accidentally met someone who changed the entire course of your life.

Your life is composed of such near accidents. At any moment, you can make a decision that completely changes your life.

There is a term for such critical moments: *inflection points*. An inflection point is a moment in which the normal rules no longer apply. In which the amazing and incredible are more likely to occur. In which you can suddenly enter a different world.

Look around you. When you hear stories of people who did the impossible, they were able to take advantage of such inflection points.

How else could a college dropout suddenly become the world's leading tech visionary?

How else could a drug and gambling addict who had never cooked in his life somehow become an acclaimed celebrity chef?

These transformations do not occur normally. Yet they can and do occur.

Moreover, they are occurring far more often now. No doubt, you are aware that the world is currently going through massive changes. We are witnessing the rise of artificial intelligence. Quantum physics is uncovering strange and surprising truths about the universe.

We are even seeing seismic shifts in our own lives. Women are upending traditional roles. Old ways of looking at the world are being radically and completely transformed.

In short, our world is entering an inflection point. And because of this fact, you are more likely to encounter an inflection point in your own life. You are more likely to suddenly enter a completely new world.

Perceptive people are realizing that this is happening. They are taking full advantage of these once-in-a-lifetime opportunities.

So how can you guarantee that you will participate in such great change?

It helps to understand the true nature of inflection points. Somehow, during such specific moments, the entire universe aligns so that the impossible becomes possible.

If you look carefully, you can comprehend what is happening. During inflection points, this is what is given to select people: *the ability to manifest powerfully*.

This explains why manifestation works for certain people but not others. This explains why, in your own life, you haven't managed to consistently manifest.

We know that manifestation is real. We have seen and heard of countless cases when the universe has granted people their greatest dreams.

But most people haven't been able to understand the underlying pattern.

The hidden secret is that manifestation is most powerful during inflection points. During such points, the universe is in alignment for a few select individuals. It is ready to hear their greatest wishes.

Moreover, such inflection points can occur at any moment.

When you are at a bar with friends, you might suddenly meet the person you have been waiting for your entire life.

When you are in a bookstore, you might abruptly see the words that open your eyes to extraordinary opportunities.

When you are at the coffee shop, they might unexpectedly mix up your order—with the order of the person who turns out to be your greatest mentor.

You don't know when you will encounter an inflection point. You don't know when your life will completely change.

But there is a way to attract such inflection points and make them more plentiful in your life. This book is about how to attract and take full advantage of these special moments.

In fact, there is a specific shortcut that will attract inflection points like moths to a flame. And that shortcut exists in the multiverse.

What is the multiverse, exactly?

You have no doubt seen or heard about the multiverse. It is now a common topic in books and movies.

The multiverse is the idea that infinite universes exist. And each universe has its own unique rules and events.

You might have seen movies in which characters suddenly pop into these other universes.

In a typical story, a character meets another version of herself. This version grew up in an alternate universe, with completely different influences and life events.

As a result, this alternate version offers profound new wisdom and knowledge to the character. Wisdom that dramatically changes the character's life.

Everyone has heard such stories. However, there is one secret about the multiverse that most people don't know.

This is the secret: *the multiverse is real.*

There are, in fact, countless universes out there. And because there are infinite universes, there are infinite variations of you.

Out there, in the multiverse, there are versions of you who took the other path. Who encountered completely new mentors and opportunities.

Out there, in the multiverse, there is an alternate reality in which you are the CEO of a major fashion company. Another in which you are an acclaimed author. Another in which you are a social media star.

Again, these are not possibilities. These are not mere conjectures. These are actual realities in which your life took a completely different course.

In fact, the latest developments in quantum mechanics have proven that the multiverse actually exists. That there are infinite universes out there. And as a result, every possibility has occurred and will occur.

And because there are infinite versions of you, there are many versions of you who have unlocked the secrets of manifestation. They know how to attract inflection points. They know how to manifest at powerful levels.

Here is the other secret to the multiverse. One that many people have already begun using to change their entire lives. *The secret is that you can connect with the other versions of yourself.*

Think about what this means. What if you could tap into the wisdom of your other selves, the ones who have achieved extraordinary happiness and success? The ones who know what to do. The ones who have figured out the secrets of the universe.

Many people have already tapped into such incredible wisdom. This is why so many strange and unexpected things are occurring right now.

The reality star who somehow becomes a powerful politician. The struggling saleswoman who suddenly comes up with an ingenious invention. The forgotten artist who abruptly achieves worldwide recognition.

All of these are happening because we are entering a new age in which everything is changing. And in these times, there are more inflection points, more opportunities to tap into the powers of the multiverse.

You can take advantage of these possibilities. Now is your time to seize the initiative.

In fact, you have always been aware of your other selves. Haven't you had moments when you felt other versions of you, somewhere out there? It was just a feeling, but nevertheless it felt very real to you.

These feelings are a sign, an indication that you have the ability to connect with the other versions of yourself. Over the course of this book, you will learn how to strengthen these connections.

These connections will reveal everything. The truth is that attracting inflection points is a subtle and complex process. Like so many things in life, it must be lived in order to be understood.

However, you can understand these truths more quickly and easily by connecting with your other selves. By learning through their examples.

In Part 1 of this book, we will delve more deeply into how you can connect with your other selves.

In Part 2, we will examine the specific approaches and mindsets that attract inflection points.

In Part 3, we will learn by applying the lessons in this book to select scenarios.

And in the conclusion, we will outline a specific course of action that will allow you to attract more inflection points in your life.

Through this process, you will realize that it is true: your life can change at any moment. Suddenly, in an instant, you can be granted the supreme power—the ability to manifest your greatest wishes and desires.

Part 1

The Multiverse

SO THEN THE QUESTION IS, HOW EXACTLY CAN YOU USE THE multiverse to achieve your goals and dreams?

This is the answer: it can give you the most important resource in the world.

There is a commonly held belief that successful people win because they are born luckier and more talented. That these people magically pick up things faster with very little effort. That they never struggle and never experience hardships like the rest of us.

However, you will come to see that this belief is wrong. In fact, there is only one factor that separates successful people from unsuccessful people: access to mentors.

But not just any mentors. The right mentors who exactly understand your dreams. Who know the easiest and most effective ways to solve all your problems. Who let you know what to do or if you are going in the wrong direction.

The truth is, you already have so many of the tools it takes to become successful. You are determined and driven. You want to achieve great things in life and not settle like society wants you to. You have unique potential inside of you that has yet to be unleashed.

The right mentor knows how to unleash your potential. She can show you how to hone your specific talents. With such precise coaching, your entire life can change. With the right mentor, everything in life will click and make more sense.

Fortunately, you can get all the guidance you need. You can actually access this mentor through the multiverse.

Somewhere out there in the multiverse, there is a version of you who is already successful. Someone who already overcame the same hardships as you. Someone who knows how to exactly manifest her goals. Someone who achieved her dreams—*your dreams*.

She could give you such precise and extremely helpful advice *because she is you*. Better than anyone else, she understands what you want from life. She knows your hangups and issues. She comprehends where you are coming from and how the world has been unfair to you.

Through the wonders of the multiverse, you can access this alternate self who possesses the knowledge and resources you have long been missing. You no longer have to feel lost, alone, and worried.

All you have to do is connect with this alternate self. To understand how this is possible, you have to comprehend one important quantum mechanics concept: *quantum entanglement*.

Quantum entanglement is an extremely strange scientific phenomenon. It seems both supernatural and mystical. However, scientific experiments have consistently verified it.

At its most basic level, it holds that when particles become connected, they stay connected. Even when they become separated by vast distances, they are still connected in some way. This connection is famously referred to by Albert Einstein as "spooky action at a distance."

That means you aren't on this journey alone. Out there in the multiverse, there are countless versions of you. And you are still connected to all of them. Including the version of you who has already achieved the success and happiness you want. The version who knows how to attract inflection points.

On some instinctive level, you can feel her. Just as long-lost twins can still feel each other's presence, you can do the same.

You are now beginning to comprehend the full power of the multiverse. You didn't know that you had such a powerful, life-affirming support system. But you do.

With the wisdom and support of your alternate selves, you will be able to transform your life. In the following chapters, we will discuss how you can begin to tap into the full power of the multiverse and learn from your alternate selves.

Chapter 1

Your Alternate Selves

THE GREATEST GIFT A MENTOR CAN GIVE YOU IS THE ABILITY TO see beyond your present conceptions of the world. You have trouble manifesting your dreams because your vision is too clouded. You are too stuck in the reality that has been given to you by society.

To achieve your dreams, you need to forget past conceptions of yourself.

Don't limit yourself to past ideas of who you thought you were. Open your mind and heart to the multiverse.

Dare to dream of completely new possibilities and wonders.

What you need are guides who can open your mind. Fortunately, you have such guides. In fact, you have an infinite number of them. They are out there in the multiverse, waiting to help you.

And there is one specific alternate self who would be particularly empowering. Out of all your alternate selves, she knows you best. She knows exactly how you have been hurting. She knows how trapped and lost you sometimes feel.

This version also knows exactly how to solve all your problems. *She knows this because she is your Future Self.*

This is true because, as Albert Einstein discovered, time is fluid. It can flow faster or slower in different universes. This means that there is an alternate universe years ahead of our own. A universe in which there is a version of you who was in the same exact place you are in now. With the same exact challenges and hardships. With only the resources and knowledge you have now.

And from this same initial position, this alternate self found her way to her dreams—*your dreams.*

Take time to fully understand what this means. It means that it is possible to resolve all your difficulties. Because a version of you already has. A version of you knows exactly what you need to do.

So how can you begin to connect with your alternate self? How can you begin opening your mind?

The first step in opening your mind is deeply reflecting on the following five truths:

1. It is possible to solve all your troubles.
2. You live in a world of infinite possibilities.
3. You have countless versions of yourself in the multiverse.
4. You are still connected to them on a mystical level according to the laws of physics.
5. At least one alternate self knows how to solve all your problems.

There are also specific exercises that will allow you to connect with your alternate self. Here is one particularly helpful exercise. When you have a quiet moment, free of any stress or distraction, close your eyes and visualize your Future Self.

Picture your Future Self as precisely and vividly as possible. Do not see her as a mere possibility. See her for who she actually is—a living, breathing person. Someone who is as human as you. Someone who has overcome all your difficulties and reached your greatest dreams.

Specifically, visualize the Future Self who is five years into your future. What does she look like? What is she wearing? Where is she living?

Visualize her home exactly. The home that you want to obtain in your own future. For example, many people dream of a house next to the beach. If this is true for you, picture the spacious room where your alternate self is sitting. See the bright sun shining through your large, floor-to-ceiling windows. Listen for the faint cries of the seagulls outside. Picture it exactly in your mind's eye.

Also look carefully at your Future Self. You see your face, but the eyes reveal a more evolved spirit. A bold and undeniable spirit.

Note her utter calmness. She feels no worry or regret. You can tell she does not stay up at night preoccupied with any anxious thoughts. She always feels a sense of utter confidence and conviction.

This alternate self has fully mastered the practice of manifestation. She knows how to get the universe to hear her. She can visualize so powerfully that she inevitably fulfills her greatest desires.

And you can learn from her. You can commune with her. See the world the way she sees it. Learn to see the world with her confidence and conviction.

Feel the raw power of her confidence. It is a palpable presence. It is like being close to a bright, warm light.

If she could talk to you, what would she say? What would she convey to you?

Look directly into your Future Self's eyes. See her absolute conviction as she tells you:

Always know that I believe in you. With all my heart and soul, I believe in you and your dreams. Know that I have seen what you have seen. Felt what you have felt. Suffered as you have suffered. And just like you, I have only gotten stronger. Someday, you will be me. You will feel my confidence. My certainty. And during this journey, I will always be by your side, giving you my support and my strength.

If you felt a small jolt when your alternate self said these words, then you are beginning your connection with your alternate self.

Right now, start with this daily exercise: at least once a day, sit in a quiet space and reach out to your alternate self. Visualize her warm face. Visualize her eyes that blaze with absolute confidence. Eyes that know you will succeed. That know you have something special within you that will keep you safe and protected.

As you get to higher stages, you will be able to connect with your alternate self throughout each hour of the day. Even in moments of extreme stress and pain, you will be able to feel her warm, comforting presence.

As you open yourself to this connection more and more, your life will change. You will become braver, more confident, and more inspired. You will see the world in new ways. You will begin to attract inflection points.

In the upcoming chapters, you will be introduced to more of your alternate selves. Each has something to teach you: a unique event, thought, or action that will lead you down paths different from your own. Paths that result in new experiences and insights.

With their support and help, you will learn how to take your manifestation practice to the next level. Through their examples, you will learn how to conquer all the things that have been interfering with your manifestation, such as doubt and fear. You will begin to fully open your mind.

Chapter 2

The Fiery Self

IT IS A FACT THAT THERE ARE INFINITE UNIVERSES AND INFINITE versions of you. Every possibility is realized in the multiverse.

At this moment, visualize yourself in one of those alternate universes. See yourself walking through its version of the Louvre Museum in Paris, France. Look at the masterpieces from the world's greatest artists lining the walls.

However, in this museum, something is different. There is one particular exhibit that stands out, even among these great works. Throngs of excited visitors breathlessly wait hours to see it.

Out of curiosity, you go to that exhibit, and you instantly realize why it is so popular. The artist's exhibit is reminiscent of the great Mexican artist Frida Kahlo. However, it is somehow bolder and filled with more passion.

When you stare at the bright, glowing paintings, you feel completely alive. You feel strong and powerful. As if you could take on any challenge.

You gaze at the artist's self-portraits, and you suddenly recognize her face. It is your face. This artist is your alternate self. And she has become the greatest artist of her generation.

Surprisingly, your alternate self forged such a fabulous career even though she grew up in a family that didn't encourage art or creativity. In fact, she grew up in poverty.

At the age of twelve, she saw her family lose nearly everything. The house. The cars. The bank accounts. And for several desperate years, her family lived on the edge of homelessness.

But something remarkable happened in the face of those bleak circumstances. Your other self realized a certain truth. She noticed that even through the worst events, she could remain strong, fierce, and determined. That no matter what the world did, it couldn't make her weak and uncertain.

And because of this startling insight, your other self entered into an inflection point.

Even at a young age, she knew exactly what she wanted to manifest: an uncommon life. She didn't want to be basic or ordinary. She wanted to do something truly amazing with her life.

And the universe granted her this wish.

Even though she had no formal training, she won a scholarship to a prominent art school. There, she became known for pushing boundaries, and all quickly came to admire (and even envy) her fearless and adventurous spirit.

While still in art school, she gained national prominence by smashing preconceived notions of femininity. Every time society told her she couldn't do certain things, she proved them wrong. She dropped out of art school. She dated whomever she wanted. She lived wherever she desired. Her art career kept taking unconventional and breathtaking turns.

Even when she failed, she laughed in response. And because she laughed, she was able to conquer every setback. When her art studio burned down, she started over again in a small New York loft. From that space, she kept making art her way according to her own rules. She was continually able to manifest her dreams.

By the time she reached her midthirties, she was widely acknowledged as one of the most talented artists of all time. Her gallery openings were covered by national newspapers and magazines from *Time* magazine to the *New York Times*. Her artwork inspired both memes and serious academic discussions. People across generations were inspired by her art because it spoke to their deep need for freedom, nonconformity, and defiance of the system. Everyone loved her.

✶ ✶ ✶

This is your alternate self. This is someone who demonstrates your true potential.

You will find that if you reflect upon her life story, you will gain powerful insights. You will learn how to live and manifest at higher levels.

What specific lessons can you learn from your alternate self's life story?

You will recall that even in the face of setbacks, your other self merely laughed. For example, when her art studio burned down, she just laughed and started over again.

This was how she was able to manifest so powerfully. It is a central tenet of manifestation that we manifest what we are thinking. When we dwell in sadness and grief, the universe sends us more things to feel sad about.

However, in that terrible moment when her art studio burned down, your other self did something extraordinary: she laughed.

And because she laughed, the universe sent her things that brought more joy and laughter, such as greater success and more artistic breakthroughs.

But for many people, her reaction seems impossible. How could someone laugh in the face of severe setbacks?

This is the answer: your view of your future is the most important thing in the world.

If you think your future is doomed, then you will always be afraid. If you are unsure if you will win, then any setback will fill you with doubt and despair.

But if you know for sure that you will ultimately win, then you will be able to do anything. You will also be able to laugh at any setback.

Knowing that you will win requires no proof. It requires no approval from the outside world. All it requires is an utter belief in yourself and your abilities.

This attitude is what makes your other self so powerful. She knows that she can conquer any setback. That she will always be okay.

This is the reason she can dare to do things her own way. She could drop out of art school and still go on to become an acclaimed artist. She could also date whomever she wanted and live however she pleased.

In other words, your other self is completely free. And she was able to achieve such freedom because she knew she would always win. That made her fearless in the face of failure. She didn't worry about the future because she knew she had an inner strength that would always sustain her. A strength that could outlast any obstacle.

You may not know it, but you also possess such phenomenal inner strength.

Look back on your own life. Think about all the challenges and setbacks you have endured. Throughout your life, you have displayed uncommon strength and determination. You have repeatedly shown that you are as strong as your other self.

However there is a crucial difference: your other self is always aware of her strength. Because of this awareness, your other self lives free from fear.

Then the question is, how can you live with greater awareness of your strength and power?

Unfortunately, the world keeps sending us things that make us forget our strength. It keeps judging our actions. Keeps overlooking what we do. Keeps pointing out every flaw and mistake. Keeps highlighting every horrible possibility.

No wonder we forget our strength and believe the worst about ourselves. It is difficult to defy the world and claim our authentic strength and power.

However, you can claim your power. It begins by continually focusing on the greatest parts of yourself, such as your undying strength and determination.

Whenever you need to access your inner strength, your Fiery Self is here to help you. She will guide you into developing an empowering mindset.

At this moment, visualize your other self in the bright, colorful interior of her artist studio. Against the backdrop of her evocative paintings, she sits, gazing at you.

You can see the fierceness in her eyes. Her uncompromising expression is both challenging and yet beautiful.

You realize here is someone unafraid to live. Someone who refuses to be intimidated by anything or anyone.

Meet her fierce but yet loving gaze and hear her as she speaks:

> Know that you have something inside you that is greater than any challenge or obstacle. You have my strength. My fierceness. My independence. My love of life.

> These are the things that will always keep you safe. That will triumphantly answer every challenge. You can always rest assured that everything will be okay.

I know you inside and out. I have seen the strength that you display on a daily basis. I know all your pain and heartache.

I have seen everything, and I admire you so much. You have my deepest respect.

I ask you now to live with this awareness. Live knowing your strength and power. With this awareness, you will be able to move mountains. You will be able to reach destinations beyond your imagination.

And I will be at your side throughout this journey. Together, we will conquer the world and forge the life that you have always wanted and deserved.

As often as possible, take time to connect with your alternate self. Feel her warm, comforting presence in your life. Hear her voice reminding you of your strength and power. Always know that you are not alone.

Chapter 3

The Brilliant Self

THERE IS AN ALTERNATE VERSION OF YOU WHO BECAME A SCIentist. And not just any scientist. Someone so brilliant that she redefined what it means to be a scientist. She became a global icon, the first scientist to win three Nobel prizes. Her beautiful mind was featured on the covers of *Vanity Fair*, *Harper's Bazaar*, and *Vogue*. Among her dazzling accomplishments was the reversal of global warming on her planet.

You might think this is impossible. You might have done poorly in your chemistry and biology classes in high school. You might even hate math. However, this is indisputably true: there is a version of you who learned how to be brilliant.

This is how it came to be. Your other self didn't set out to be a scientist. In fact, she grew up with a severe learning disability, which made it difficult for her to read and write. As a result of that disability, people consistently dismissed her. Told her that learning was impossible for people like her. Even her parents told her that she had no potential and that college would be a waste for her.

And your other self believed them. She believed she had no

worth and her entire life would be limited. She thought she would always be stunted, like a twisted tree that had to grow on barren soil.

As a result, your other self was always consumed by doubt. Even when she tried to study, there was always a voice in her mind that told her things such as, "You can't do it. You shouldn't even try."

This might have been her entire life, but fortunately, the universe sends us inflection points to guide us to another path. And your other self encountered such an inflection point through a teacher. He opened her mind by asking her a simple question: "Why do you listen to your doubts?"

And through that inflection point, your other self suddenly felt enlightened. She realized her doubts were merely doubts, and they indicated no truth about herself or her abilities. It didn't matter if her former teachers or even her parents fed those doubts. Doubts were always shadows to be dismissed.

This momentous realization changed everything.

It allowed her to manifest for the first time in her life. And she manifested the one thing she always wanted: to make a difference in the world.

Now that she was suddenly free of all doubts, the universe granted her wish, and she began to dramatically improve. She shocked everyone by becoming the best student in her high school. And she further surprised them by gaining admission to Harvard.

There, she impressed everyone with her growing brilliance. While still an undergraduate, she conducted groundbreaking research into the science of global warming.

Then your other self went to the most prestigious graduate program in the nation. Leading professors clamored to be her research advisor. Everyone respected her. They were awed by her ability to take apart existing ideas and point out all the flaws that no one else had noticed. The way that her mind would suddenly leap to unconventional and extraordinary connections.

Men became enraptured by her beautiful mind, and women were awed by her. People breathlessly followed her every step. They wondered how she could achieve so many things. She regularly made breakthroughs in research while becoming a fashion icon. She became the first person to show the entire world that smart was sexy.

No one understood the source of her brilliance. They were just mesmerized by the way she thought. The way she spoke. The way she moved the world with her ideas. At every turn, they didn't know what to expect from her.

Not surprisingly, your other self set out to do the impossible. Most importantly, she conceived ingenious new ways to reverse global warming. To heal the ailing forests and oceans.

No one could stop her. Not even the oil and energy companies who were threatened by her innovations. To discredit her, they marshaled billions of dollars. And with those billions, they hired their own scientists and heavily influenced politicians.

A typical person would have been overwhelmed with doubt at this moment. But your other self was not a typical person. She knew the secret: that doubts are just thoughts without substance. That they are not reflections of reality.

With this secret, your other self continued to manifest at extraordinary levels. At every step, she was like the clever fox who always found a way to outwit the hounds nipping at her heels. She exposed the attempts to fire her. She systematically destroyed the false arguments and lies thrown against her. And she persuaded the public of the truth of her words and ideas. In this manner, she utterly defeated all the forces arrayed against her.

Her achievements brought her the adoration of billions. Her

every word and action was followed by countless people. In particular, she inspired a new generation of young women who also realized that they, too, were without limits. Her beautiful mind altered the fate of her entire world.

※ ※ ※

This is your alternate self, and she demonstrates your true potential.

She reveals what you can accomplish once you conquer your doubts.

Your other self's key insight was that her doubts were not real. They were only thoughts. They were not signs from the universe that something bad was going to occur. They only have power because we pay attention to them.

At this moment, just consider this scenario. Over the coming months and years, you follow the example of your alternate self. Every time doubts pop up in your mind, you ignore them completely. Instead, you focus all your attention on the extraordinary opportunities the world has to offer. How will your life unfold?

According to the laws of manifestation, the universe will reward you. It will keep sending you things that inspire even more joy and confidence in your life.

In this manner, you can see how you can manifest at an extraordinary level. When you do encounter an inflection point, and you react with such calm focus, you will be able to manifest nearly anything.

You see the power of your focus. Whatever you focus on becomes large in your mind. Your focus is like a magnifying glass. It increases the size of whatever it is aimed at.

Therefore, when you focus on your doubts, they become the largest things in your mind. And the universe will send you things that inspire even more doubt.

To manifest, you have to free yourself from your doubts. You need to shift your attention away from them.

But how can you do this? How can you ignore your doubts when they are so loud and insistent?

For example, your doubts might tell you that you can't do things. They tell you that you will never succeed. That you just aren't good enough. That you can never trust yourself. That you are alone with your problems.

In such instances, you can focus on something else: your Brilliant Self.

At this moment, focus on her. She is seated, watching you. Her expression is warm, soothing, and even affectionate.

When she speaks, her voice is yours. But there is a musical quality to it. A comforting tone that reminds you that everything will be okay.

Her melodious voice rings in your ears as she speaks:

I know you. I know you completely. I know how strong you are. I know your light, your love of life, your toughness.

Listen to me as I tell you that you are good enough. You will succeed, and you can completely trust yourself. Let yourself feel the complete depths of your drive, talent, and determination.

I understand your doubts, and I know how painful and real they seem. But remember, your doubts are not real. Your doubts are nothing compared to your strength. I will show you how to make your doubts as quiet as a bare whisper.

You are also not alone. I am always here, by your side. Together, we will unlock your true potential. You will realize all the amazing things you are capable of. I will show you the wonders of the world.

As often as possible, be aware of your alternate self's bright presence in your life. Be aware that someone out there understands you. Is always cheering you onward. Knows that you can succeed.

In moments of doubt, listen for her warm, melodious voice. Feel the connection between you two. That connection alone is enough to remind you that you are stronger than your doubts.

Over time, you will find her confidence and certainty spilling over into your own life. Things will get easier for you. The universe will begin to see and hear you, just as it sees and hears your alternate self.

Chapter 4

The Calm Self

YOU ARE IN AN ALTERNATE WORLD, AND YOU ARE BROWSING television channels. You aren't expecting much. Just the same old tedious entertainment shows that seem to clutter the airwaves.

However, you suddenly find something startlingly different. You find a talk show in which the host says something so profound that it pierces your very soul.

And you suddenly get it. You suddenly understand how to finally let go of all your fears and how to forever calm all your anxieties and worries.

It is a revelatory moment, so profound that it takes you a moment to recognize the face of the host. It is your face, or specifically the face of one of your alternate selves.

Because you have an alternate self out there in the multiverse who discovered the secret of utter calm and peace. And she went on to change her entire world as the greatest speaker and talk show host of all time.

This is how your other self came to fulfill her grand destiny.

At first, you would not have expected her to become such an inspiring and charismatic figure. She was extremely shy and insecure when she was young. So overwhelmed with fear and anxiety that she could barely leave her home.

But then one morning, she decided she had had enough. She realized she could not live the rest of her life like this. Anything had to be better than being a prisoner of her fears.

Later that day, as she attended her college class, she noticed something for the first time. There in the classroom was a pamphlet detailing Buddhist monasteries in the Far East. On the cover was an illustration of the Buddha himself, sitting calmly with a soft smile, completely at peace with the world.

In that instant, your other self made an audacious decision—one that went against everything she had been taught. She decided to quit college and go to the Far East on her own.

When she made this choice, she felt her world shift, as if everything was suddenly in alignment. And she attracted an inflection point.

In that moment, your other self manifested her greatest wish: *to live free from fear*. And the universe saw and heard her. It granted her wish.

When your other self traveled to the Far East, she stumbled upon a hidden monastery. There, she was fortunate to find a great teacher who taught her how to completely master her fears.

All she had to do was follow a method that had worked for thousands of years: consciously relax all her muscles and slowly breathe in and out while calmly waiting for her fears to fade from her mind.

It was such a simple method, but it gave her the peace she had always longed for. She threw herself into mastering it. Day and night, whenever worry and anxiety clouded her mind, she consciously applied this miraculous technique.

Your other self changed dramatically once she began freeing herself from her fears. She became bolder and more charismatic.

Even the other monks commented on how she developed an inner glow that made her beautiful and graceful.

In time, your other self realized she had something important to teach the world, so she left the monastery as suddenly as she had entered it. And she returned to society a dramatically changed person.

At first, it was challenging. She had no money or resources. Just her calm, graceful presence. But it was enough. She quickly began to attract followers. They were drawn to the beauty of her powerful mind and soul. She radiated an alluring glow that made everyone want to be near her. In particular, her eyes captivated them. Eyes that seemed so knowing and full of wisdom. Eyes that seemed to pierce people's souls.

Wherever your other self went, she changed people's lives. Anxious and fearful mothers learned how to be cool and serene. Young women who lived every day in fear learned how to be bold, confident, and accepting.

At first, she taught to only small crowds. But they soon grew in number. Strange things seemed to always occur in these gatherings. One time, a man suddenly realized the meaning of his life, and he hurried home to give his wife the love and affection she had always needed. Another time, a woman abruptly realized she didn't need to stay in an abusive relationship—she had the capacity to be happy and free on her own.

Everywhere your other self went, she set people free. Because fear no longer held them, they realized they could lead the lives they had always wanted.

Inevitably, news of her life-changing presence and ideas spread. Larger and larger crowds gathered to hear her speak. Many of her admirers sought to give her even bigger stages. They arranged for her to have her own show, where she could broadcast her truths to the entire world. Soon that show became one of the most popular across the globe.

However, many in society found her dangerous. Some accused her of corrupting existing religions. Others were alarmed at her message. How she affirmed the power of the individual to live free of fear and restraint. How she made people harder to control and manipulate.

Some countries banned her show. In other countries, authorities tried to take her off the airwaves and the internet.

But your other self could not be denied. By this point, she had completely mastered herself. It didn't matter when others threatened to destroy all that she had built. Nor did it matter that she might lose all her followers.

Those were just fears, and your other self did as she always did: she calmly relaxed herself and waited for all those anxieties and worries to dissipate from her mind. They always did, just as she knew that they would. And this made her powerful beyond measure.

While authorities could ban her show, they couldn't ban her message and influence. People still covertly watched her show and her videos. Her followers created secret societies and organizations that numbered in the millions.

And your other self marshaled all her vast power to stop this censorship. She used her influence to get sympathetic governments to plead her case in front of the United Nations. She persuaded her most powerful followers to join forces across the entire planet. She could not be denied. Her presence was too empowering, beautiful, and captivating.

She was like a force of nature. She continued to spread her message in the face of all opposition. And over time, she created a world in which people had the power to free themselves from fear. People could choose the lives they wanted, without any worry or anxiety. It became the world that everyone had always desired—one defined by complete freedom, peace, and happiness.

※ ※ ※

This is your other self. She demonstrates your full potential.

She can help you master one of the most powerful abilities in the world: calmness.

Many people wouldn't think of calmness as a superpower, but it is. It is what allows you to manifest at a high level.

Once you master calmness, you become a force of nature, as still and powerful as water. Water may not seem like a potent force, but over time it can break granite and carve mountains. The immense Grand Canyon is an example of what water can accomplish over time.

When you are calm, the world cannot hurt you.

When you are calm, you can conquer the mental blocks that prevent you from wholeheartedly putting your thoughts and dreams out into the universe.

When you are calm, you can unlock your creativity, and you will be able to invent completely new solutions to your problems.

If you are calm when you encounter an inflection point, you will be able to manifest everything you ever wanted or needed. You will truly be able to lead an extraordinary life.

You might wonder, how can we remain calm in the face of strong emotions, such as fear?

Our fears often seem overwhelming. It sometimes feels as if our lives will suddenly fall apart at any moment. As if something horrible is about to occur, and we are helpless to prevent it.

But it is always possible to become the calm center of the storm. It is always possible to stand strong and serenely dismiss even your darkest fears.

When you are in the midst of overwhelming, negative emotions, visualize your Calm Self. She will guide you to your inner calmness.

See her seated in a lotus position, as calm as the Buddha himself. Observe how she relaxes every muscle in her body.

In watching her, you feel your own muscles relax. In particular, your neck and shoulder muscles loosen. You feel as relaxed as if you had spent all day at a luxurious spa.

Observe her breathe slowly in and out.

You follow her example. With each slow, deep breath you release all your fears, anxieties, and frustrations. Each breath leaves you feeling clean and whole.

Observe her patiently wait.

You do the same. You let every negative thought and emotion slowly dissipate from your mind and body. You allow yourself to be as calm as a cool, still pond.

Meet your other self's gaze. See the infinite patience, love, and sympathy in her beautiful eyes. You feel as if you are in the presence of someone who understands you completely. And she loves and forgives you wholeheartedly.

Hear her as she speaks:

> I know that you sometimes stay up at night, worried that your future will turn out badly. Worried that everything will go wrong. The fear is so bad that it's all you see.

> But I am here to tell you that everything will work out. Trust in the universe. Trust in my words and my example. You have something special within you. A strength that can and will not be denied. Don't worry. The universe has greater plans for you.

You have the power to let go of your fears and worries. You just have to see and embrace this power. I know you have this ability because I have it as well.

You have it within you to be at peace. You can accept the love, forgiveness, and kindness of the universe. You do not have to worry—you are enough.

Become like water. When the world gets loud with its taunts and tries to scare you with worries, let everything slowly drift away. Your calmness can transcend everything. You can defeat anything.

Even during your darkest moments, you can always see your alternate self's relaxed form, seated in a lotus position. You can see how she slowly breathes in and out. You can see how she calmly waits.

Realize you also have this power. You are also powerful beyond measure.

Chapter 5

The Confident Self

THE ROOM IS ENORMOUS AND ORNATE. THE CEILINGS ARE gilded with real gold, and multimillion-dollar paintings line the walls. There is a gigantic table made of the rarest and most expensive wood in the middle of this cavernous room.

Seated around the table are the most powerful business people on the planet. This is an alternate world, but you recognize many of the faces. They are multibillionaires in your own world as well. Individuals who changed everything by creating extraordinary inventions and companies. Who ruthlessly made billions of dollars in their pursuit of power and influence.

But there is one person who clearly stands out even among these enormously powerful individuals. Her eyes blaze with supernatural confidence. Her posture is more regal than royalty. Her words ring throughout the giant room like thunder.

And only then do you recognize this exceptional person. It is your alternate self.

How did your other self reach the pinnacle of wealth and power? How did she accumulate over five hundred billion dollars?

The answer lies in your other self's humble roots. She grew

up dirt poor. So poor that her family lived in a tiny trailer home. One about the size of a prison cell. One so old and broken down that its walls were stained with orange rust and black mold. And everyone in their town looked down on her uneducated, impoverished family.

Your other self grew up feeling scared and ashamed. Every day, she saw the contempt and disdain in the eyes of others. They seemed to say, "You are nothing. Less than dirt. Not worth a second of our time."

Even in school, she knew she was the poorest and worst student. She walked from class to class with her head down, hoping no one would notice her. And when they did notice her, she felt their ridicule and scorn down to her very soul. Every minute of her life, she was aware she was lesser than other people.

But then one day while reading a book in a library, she stumbled upon one life-changing sentence: "Confidence is a choice; it is something you can seize at any point in your life. You do not have to wait."

Suddenly, something clicked in her mind. It was as if the entire world made sense for the first time in her life.

She realized she had been waiting her entire life for permission to feel confident, to feel good about herself. But what if the book was right, and she didn't have to wait?

That was when she made the decision to be confident right here, right now. And when she made this bold choice, the universe saw her.

It also heard her as she manifested her greatest desire: to be the most successful person in the world. And the universe gave her a path to this dream.

From then on, your other self lived differently. She no longer waited for the world to give her permission. Instead, she chose to walk with her head held high. To project an air of self-assurance.

She was shocked by the results. People began to treat her differently. They still noticed her secondhand clothing and the fact that her family was one of the poorest in the entire town. But they treated her with respect. Once she acted as if she belonged, everyone treated her accordingly.

She felt as if she had stumbled onto a great secret. She had once believed that confidence was reserved for a select few. But now she realized it was a secret power that she could grab at will.

She began doing things she had thought impossible. She boldly walked into stores asking for jobs, and against all odds, a clothing boutique hired her. There, she became the top salesperson. She realized she had to simply look each customer in the eye and confidently tell them the article of clothing looked wonderful on them. And then they almost always bought the item.

It was an amazing and intoxicating power. After some time at the clothing boutique, she secured an internship at a software company. Even though she was the only non-college graduate in her division, she again became the top salesperson. Her air of utter self-assurance made her irresistible to others. Customers fell under her spell. Coworkers wanted to be around her.

Even when your other self encountered setbacks, she refused to let them shake her confidence. Once, her boss unfairly blamed her for losing one of their biggest accounts. Such an incident would have devastated most people.

However, your other self knew that as long as she chose to be confident, the world would eventually turn in her favor. And that is exactly what happened. Her boss was fired, and she was promoted to his position.

Your other self kept moving on to bigger and better things. And eventually she began working for the largest companies in the world. But this wasn't enough for your other self. She wanted more.

Over the course of her stellar career, she had gathered a network of the best and brightest. All of whom deeply admired her bold and confident spirit. She met personally with each great scientist, engineer, and businessperson. She looked them in the eye and promised that together, they would change the entire world. And they believed her.

She assembled the greatest collection of minds the world had ever seen. Together, they set out to do the impossible: create a new source of clean energy. This was a brand-new technology her world desperately needed. With it, countless problems would be instantly solved.

However, there were numerous skeptics. Many openly ridiculed your other self in international publications. They called her naive and even crazy. Some were openly misogynistic, proclaiming it was impossible for a woman to be innovative or an industry leader.

Nevertheless, not even the cruelest comment could rattle your other self. She always chose to be confident, even when the entire world seemed to turn against her.

Because of her boldness, she had a knack for inspiring others. When her scientists and engineers struggled to create new ideas and solutions, she always made herself present. With just a smile, wink, or nod, she encouraged them to achieve greatness. She would say things such as, "For people like us, nothing is truly impossible." And no one could resist her audacious yet warm smile.

She raised billions of dollars to keep her company going. But her company burned through billions of dollars as well. Over time, her critics became louder. Many wanted her to step down and "let a man take over."

Things became bad enough that the company was on the brink of collapse, and she was in danger of losing everything.

At this point, most people would have hit rock bottom and given up. However, your other self was not like most people.

Because of her supreme confidence, she attracted an inflection point—a pivotal moment that brought her one step closer to achieving her dream.

In that instant, she shone like the sun. The universe recognized her daring presence, her declaration to the world that she'd never give up. It gave her the power to manifest her greatest wish.

And then it happened. Her company made an enormous breakthrough. They invented a new source of clean energy.

Instantly, everything changed. The same publications that had ridiculed her now proclaimed her a genius and visionary. Everyone showered her with adoration. Every newspaper and magazine across the globe featured her on its cover. Social media buzzed with admiration for her audacity and vision.

Soon your other self became the wealthiest person on the planet. She could have gone on to become the world's first trillionaire, but she used her wealth to make technology affordable for everyone.

She regularly traveled to outlying villages in the developing world. There, she could see what she had created.

Where there had once been shanties, there were now gleaming new buildings. Villagers always came to thank her. They told her that she had changed everything. Now they had limitless electricity and could breathe clean air. Now they could dream of a wonderful future.

In response, your other self gave them her radiant smile. She remembered the small trailer she had grown up in. And she recalled the most important moment in her life: when she made the decision to be absolutely confident in herself. That was when everything changed—her life and her entire world.

✻ ✻ ✻

This is your other self. She demonstrates your full potential.

You will notice her key insight: she didn't have to wait for the world to give her permission. She could choose to be confident right here, right now.

Many people believe they need permission from the world. They believe that they can only be confident if things are going well. If the world gives them reason to be confident.

Yet the greatest individuals did not wait for the world to give them permission. Even when they seemed to have nothing, they boldly seized their dreams. This is the example of great individuals such as Steve Jobs and Walt Disney. They started with nothing and ended up with everything.

You can do the same. You can always choose to be whomever or whatever you want. You have to realize that you possess such incredible freedom.

However, choosing to be confident can seem impossible. When things aren't going well, we are told it is a sign that success is impossible.

But deep down, you already know the magnificent truth: you were born for more than ordinary existence.

The truth is, things will work out for you. You are destined for greater things. Your setbacks aren't endings to your dreams—they're merely the universe's way of preparing you for greatness. And right now, in this very moment, your next breakthrough is taking shape, waiting for you to rise up and claim it.

Maybe today it's just looking in the mirror and giving yourself a kind smile. Tomorrow it might be speaking up in a meeting, even if your voice shakes. And yes, some days you might feel like you're faking it—like you're wearing confidence like a coat that doesn't quite fit. That's normal. That's human.

You don't have to be ready. You don't have to be perfect. You just have to be willing to take one tiny step forward, even if you're scared. Because here's the truth: your heart knows the way. Trust it, just a little bit more each day. And with each small act of courage, something remarkable begins to happen.

Each time you choose to be this confident, you increase the likelihood that you will attract an inflection point—a magical moment when you can manifest on a powerful level. Then you will be able to suddenly change your entire life.

Sometimes, this may seem hard, even impossible. Fortunately, you have a guide to inspire you, to guide you ever forward.

At this moment, visualize your Confident Self. See her standing with her shoulders back, head proudly tilted forward. See how she commands the room, her gaze bold and fearless.

Hear her as she tells you:

The time is now. Your true self emerges today. Inside you burns a fierce confidence—yes, the same fire that drives me. It's already there, waiting.

Society told you to ask permission to exist. To shrink. To doubt. To give up your dreams because they are impossible to achieve.

But no more. This way of thinking ends now.

You can feel your authentic self clawing to break free. To be seen. To be heard. Release her. Let her roar.

Feel that boldness stirring in your chest. Even if it whispers now, listen close. It's urging you to act. To try new things. To shatter your limitations.

Watch me. I'll show you what freedom looks like. What it means to be fierce, to be unstoppable. I'll teach you to silence the noise and hear your soul's truth.

Study how I move through the world. See your own magnificent potential reflected back. Because I am not separate from you—I am you. I am who you can and will be.

When you become your true, confident self, you will be able to manifest at the highest level possible. You will become loud and clear to the entire universe.

Chapter 6

The Imaginative Self

IN AN ALTERNATE UNIVERSE, YOU HAVE JUST SCORED AN EXCLUsive invitation to the Oscars!

You are so ecstatic because you've always dreamed of being invited to such an iconic event.

As you step through the entrance doors, the cinematic orchestral music fills the air. You feel as if you have been transported back to the golden age of 1930s Hollywood, which seems to be the theme this year.

You can hardly contain your excitement. Everywhere you turn, you see someone famous. In high school, you used to have posters of these celebrity crushes all over your bedroom wall. Now, you are standing literally inches away from them.

You try to play it cool and not freak out when you see Zendaya, who looks as stunning and fierce as you imagined her to be. But when you see Robert Downey Jr., you almost faint.

You try not to stare, but everyone just looks so beautiful and flawless. You suddenly feel so ordinary, so out of place. Like an imposter who doesn't belong in this upper echelon of society.

Still, you try to soak it all in and enjoy yourself. After all, you don't think you'll ever have the chance again to be around so much greatness.

But then, all of a sudden, everyone in the theater goes quiet when a certain actress enters the room.

Everyone stares at this actress. You hear whispers around the room saying how this actress is the new "it" girl of Hollywood. How she's the only actress to have multiple nominations this evening.

You wonder, who is this new actress? Who is everyone so excited to see? You wonder if you've seen her in any films lately.

But then, when you get a closer look at this actress, you are stunned to see that she has your face. Even your same nervous laughter. You think, No, it can't be.

Then the announcer opens up the envelope slowly and says, "And the Oscar for Best Actress goes to..."

Your name is called. And everyone in the entire room stands up and gives a thunderous ovation.

You suddenly realize that your alternate self is this actress who has just won the award.

As your alternate self glides up to the stage to receive this award, she gives the most memorable speech:

> I know that from the outside, my life looks magical. I'm at the Academy Awards, and I've just won an Oscar for Best Actress.
>
> But the truth is that for most of my life, I've been told that I wasn't good enough. That I wasn't leading lady material. That I wasn't beautiful enough. So many people told me to my face that I didn't have star quality.
>
> But here I am, living and breathing proof that anything is possible.

That success can happen to anyone, even to someone like me who has been rejected millions of times.

So to all the women out there who have been told no, fight for your dreams. Prove your critics wrong. Never, ever let anyone stop you from creating art.

In response to this rousing speech, Jennifer Lawrence and Emma Stone stand up and become her loudest cheering squad. Women in the room are tearing up. Even Meryl Streep, who never reacts to any acceptance speech.

This is the life of one of your alternate selves. In this universe, she actually wins the Oscar for Best Actress more than any other actor throughout film history. Her performances transform and transcend films, catapulting Hollywood into a new era of artistic creation. In this universe, she is an absolute icon.

However, your alternate self didn't start off this bold and confident. She wasn't born a star. In her past, she was actually the least likely person to make it in Hollywood.

As a child, your alternate self grappled with a noticeable stutter and a nervous tic. Bullies publicly humiliated her, cruelly imitating her stutter and tics. She hid in the background and believed her destiny was to be quiet and invisible forever.

However, she was randomly placed in a speech and drama class in seventh grade. At first, she did poorly. Her hands shook as she spoke. She got the lowest grade on every speech, almost failing the class.

Until one day, she stumbled upon a monologue. One with a phrase that changed her entire life: "You have the power to reimagine who you are."

That one line did something strange to her. It set her free.

It triggered her imagination to visualize herself as anyone she wanted to be.

When she imagined herself as queen, she felt like a queen. When she imagined herself as a rockstar, she felt an electric energy permeating throughout her entire body.

Through using her imagination, she realized she didn't have to be the shy, scared girl she had been her entire life. She could be someone new. Someone exciting. Someone who seized life by the reins.

She then did something completely out of character: she decided to stop being invisible and start becoming invincible.

And when she made such a startling choice, the universe heard her. It gave her a completely new path in life. An inflection point that allowed her to manifest her dream: to become the world's greatest actor.

The next day, your other self felt a new power brewing inside her. When she performed a monologue in class, she blew everyone away. She commanded the room. She was bold. Funny. Even charming. Never in her life had she been any of those things.

Everyone could not stop talking about her performance. How incredible she was. How they wished they could do what she just did. At that very moment, the entire school fell in love with her.

She knew right then and there *this* was what she was supposed to do for the rest of her life. Follow her dreams. Become an actress.

However, her parents didn't support her. They tried to shut down her imagination. They screamed at her, telling her she was wasting her time on a dream that would never come true.

But it was too late. Your other self already imagined big dreams. She already imagined how she wanted life to be. Nothing could stop her from pursuing this dream.

After she finished high school, she used what little savings she had on bus rides that took her to where she needed to be: Los Angeles, California.

To support herself, she worked as a waitress at a restaurant frequented by Hollywood's elite. At first, she was scared. She didn't have any connections. She didn't have any formal training. As she marveled at the starlets and producers, she wondered if she could even do it.

But every time your other self felt scared, she remembered why she was put on this earth. She was put on this earth to be a star.

So she went at this with full force. She studied acting day and night. She used her irresistible laughter to charm student directors and get parts in their films. She boldly showed up at the doors of agents and casting directors.

For some time, it was absolutely brutal. Most of the agents and casting directors never gave her a chance. They took one look at her headshot and immediately rejected her. One casting director looked her straight in the face and told her, "You don't have what it takes to be a star."

Most people would have quit with the amount of rejection your other self faced. Most people would have felt that there was no hope.

But your other self never took no for an answer. Instead of feeling devastated, she taught herself how to laugh at rejection. How to not take it personally. She knew that if she never gave up, if she kept taking chances, she would inevitably achieve her dreams.

This bold attitude guided your other self to think outside the box, especially when it came to auditioning. It inspired her to do things her own way. Do things other actors wouldn't dare do.

During one casting call, where every girl looked the same—same hair, same height, same smile—your other self came in completely different. She dyed her hair hot pink and portrayed a rebellious persona, even though casting directors were looking for someone demure and sweet.

And it worked. Your other self was cast in what was supposed to be a small role for only one episode of a new hit teenage show on Netflix. However, she was the only girl to make the lead actor (a male heartthrob of the time) blush. Their undeniable chemistry drew everyone to this show, and their one scene together went viral on TikTok with over one billion views.

Her presence enchanted the world. Everyone asked, "Who is this girl? And how can I get more of her in my life?"

The writers and directors took note of her talent and completely changed the script to feature her in every single episode. Then, she was promoted to a series regular to join the main cast.

Suddenly, everything changed. Your other self went from barely surviving on instant ramen to becoming a rising star in Hollywood. Everything she ever wanted in life started happening all at once.

In between shooting her Netflix show, she was also flying to Paris and Tokyo to film romantic comedies and action films. Her breathtaking beauty and signature flirty smile was plastered all over billboards and buses.

Your other self became America's sweetheart. The world could not get enough of her. Everything she did brought so much joy to their lives.

But soon, there was a shift in her career. Older actresses warned her it would happen to her sooner or later. That she wouldn't be young forever. That soon, Hollywood would get tired of her and give her roles to younger actresses.

And it did happen. When she hit a certain age, she was offered fewer and fewer roles. Casting directors no longer envisioned her as the leading lady. She was pressured to take small, one-dimensional parts to save her career.

However, your other self refused to accept this fate. She wouldn't let Hollywood use her and throw her away whenever they felt like it.

And through that act of defiance, through imagining a greater future for herself and all actresses, she attracted an inflection point that lifted her from the darkness.

The universe heard her loud and clear as she manifested a bold change in Hollywood. She reimagined Hollywood to celebrate all women, no matter their age, shape, or background. She wanted the world to recognize the beauty and truth in all of us.

So she sacrificed her career for something greater. To take on Hollywood. To fight the institutional forces that condemned actresses for getting older.

Your other self formed an unstoppable team of women who worked together to reimagine what films should look like. To write female characters that defied social conventions. To boldly go where no film had gone before.

Weeks leading up to the premiere of her first film, the entire Hollywood industry was against her. Critics assumed her film would flop. Even her former castmates declared that she would make the worst movie Hollywood would ever see.

But everyone was wrong.

This film was nothing like anyone had ever seen before. It was unconventional, yet so arrestingly beautiful and authentically real. The raw creative vision was unmatched.

To everyone's surprise, the film broke box office records. Although it was just a small indie movie, it ended up being the number-one movie that opening weekend. And by the end of the year, it grossed over two billion dollars, surpassing even top superhero movies.

This is how your other self swept the Oscars the following

year. She became the only woman ever to win Best Actress, Best Director, Best Screenplay, and Best Picture—all in the same night.

Because of her films, her daring vision to reimagine female empowerment, the entire world experienced a cosmic shift.

In Hollywood and beyond, men were no longer the ones in charge. They could no longer dictate the way women should look and be.

Women everywhere refused to play along with men's rules. They stopped living for society's approval. Instead, they gained the courage to dream big and achieve beyond their wildest imagination.

There was no turning back. Your alternate self became the face of a new era. One filled with refreshing progress and innovation. One where women's voices would never again be denied.

※ ※ ※

This is your other self. She demonstrates your full potential.

You will note that she began her life as a background character. Someone too shy and insecure to be noticed by anyone. Yet she transformed herself. She became bold, dynamic, and charismatic. Someone irresistible to the entire world.

Her key insight was that she could reimagine who she was. This is an uncommon belief for most people because they believe that their identities are static and fixed. They feel stuck with the identities that society has given them.

However, deep inside, you know the truth: we contain multiple layers. We can choose to be whomever we want, whenever we want. We don't have to follow society's rules.

But how can we do this? You know you have hidden depths. You can feel the boldness and charisma within you. However, it can seem impossible to let that version of you out. You may not know how to express your inner fire.

This is the answer: you can free yourself by using your powers of imagination.

But at this point, you might wonder, "How can I use my imagination to recreate my life?"

You will note that at one point, your other self made the daring decision to be completely different. Other actresses showed up to an important audition wearing the same outfit and portraying the same, predictable persona. However, your other self showed up with hot-pink hair and went totally against the script.

That is the secret. You can begin using your powers of imagination once you realize that society's rules and expectations do not have to be followed. That you can choose to disrupt the normal order.

Why didn't the other actresses act as wild and different as your other self? Because they didn't know that it was possible. They made the assumption that rules and expectations needed to be followed.

Once you begin questioning the "normal" and expected, then you will free your imagination. You will be able to imagine completely new ways to act, feel, and think.

Fortunately, you have a guide who will help you on this path. See your Imaginative Self now standing in front of you. She is beautiful and regal, with a queen's presence. But then she unexpectedly twirls around and bows down to you, with a playful smirk on her face that makes you smile.

You realize here is someone who does not feel bound by the normal rules. Here is someone who is completely free.

Hear her speak to you:

I have been where you are. I have also felt bound by society's restrictions. I thought I had no choice. I thought I could only be one person—the person who society said I was.

But I discovered that I had something inside me. An ability to envision completely new ways to act, think, and feel. It was exciting and liberating. It set me free, and it made me feel alive.

Never forget this truth: you also possess this extraordinary gift. Inside you, your imagination burns bright and runs wild like a magnificent, untamed force of nature.

Never cage it. Never apologize for its boundless spirit. For in your imagination lies the master key to every door your future holds. So embrace it fiercely. Let it lead you to undiscovered places.

With the powers of your imagination, you are completely free. With it, you can forget the past. You can forget all your regrets and fears. You have the power to imagine a completely new self. The person you always wanted to be. The person you truly are.

Through her words, you are beginning to realize that imagination has this one special ability: it is subversive. It has the power to reimagine the existing order. It dares to say that this is not how things have to be. It dares to say that you can be anything you want. It dares to say that only you can decide the course of your glorious and magnificent life.

Chapter 7

The Free-Spirited Self

YOU WAKE UP TO YOUR PHONE BUZZING. AS YOU CHECK THE notifications on your phone, a TikTok video catches your eye.

You see a woman speak directly to the camera. Her voice is a bit shaky, but she seems ready to bare her soul to the world.

She shares how, for most of her life, she thought she would amount to nothing. She was the only one of her friends and family who couldn't find a good job for many years.

For so long, she felt scared of the world. Afraid of failure. Ashamed of how far behind in life she was.

Then, her eyes are filled with tears. She looks straight at the camera, holds up a book, and says, "To whoever wrote this book, thank you. Thank you. From the bottom of my heart. You showed me how much potential I have. You set me free. Now, I have the confidence to chase my dreams."

As you scroll through TikTok, all you see are videos like hers. People from all over the world are raving about this same book. Budding entrepreneurs from Indonesia share how this book gave them the confidence to think differently. Single moms from Nigeria praise how this book gave them strength to overcome hardships.

When you peer more closely at the book they proudly hold up to the camera, you notice that it is your photo on the back cover and your name in bold on the front.

You realize that it is your alternate self who wrote this book. But it is just not any book. It is the bestselling book of all time. A book that has single-handedly changed the world. One that has freed the souls of billions of people and showed them how to live life on their own terms.

But your alternate self did not always feel so free and empowered. She actually grew up in an oppressive environment, where she was expected to follow rules, never question authority, and repress her own needs.

As a child, every morning she stared at the list of rules her mom posted on her bedroom door:

Sleep by 8:30 p.m.

No art

No playing

Listen to your parents

Must get 100 percent on all assignments

Must be two years ahead of peers

For her entire childhood, your other self lived life on a rigid schedule. Since her parents wanted full control over her education, they homeschooled her. They never gave her a vacation or a day off. From morning to night, her only companions were textbooks.

There was no fun. No laughter. Not once did she ever see her parents smile.

This was her life for many years. She felt like a prisoner in her own home.

Until one day, as she stared at the rules, she suddenly realized something. She didn't want to continue living like this.

For a long time, she had been aware that there was a huge world out there. A world in which the new and unexpected occurred. A world without oppressive rules and schedules.

She was now eighteen, and she burned to go out and explore that wild and free world.

Maybe it was the young couple she'd watched from her window yesterday, dancing in the rain without umbrellas or raincoats, their laughter startling and wonderful to her ears. Afterward, she had only been able to sit in silence, unable to forget their laughter and joy.

Now, standing in her meticulously organized room, she reached for the rules sheet. With trembling fingers, she unpinned it from her door. Then she ripped it to shreds.

In that moment when she challenged society's rules, your other self attracted an inflection point.

Suddenly, she felt acutely and intensely alive. She heard a wind chime somewhere down the street beginning to ring, and its notes aligned perfectly with the thoughts in her mind. She saw a leaf floating in the wind, swaying as if it contained a message meant only for her.

For the first time, your other self felt known, seen, recognized—not just by any one thing but by the universe itself. And in that magical moment, she manifested her greatest desire: *I want to be free.*

That day, she left her home, with all its rules, behind.

She had no plan. No resources. No contacts. However, she felt empowered, exhilarated. Everywhere she looked, she saw open roads.

Inside, her heart beat with a peculiar mix of vulnerability and invincibility. She didn't know for sure what the next day would bring, but she was not scared. For the first time in her life, she felt wonderfully and intensely alive.

Each sunrise offered her an infinite possibility. She felt an intoxicating pride in solving each day's puzzle—finding food, finding shelter, finding her way. Every day, there were small victories: a successful negotiation for a room, a meal shared with newfound friends, a safe passage to the next destination. In the wild chaos of the world, she blossomed like an exotic flower.

Eventually, through a series of odd jobs, your other self found her way to an artist commune. There, she studied how these brilliant minds created art—naturally, following the unseen rhythms of the universe, without a schedule.

Her most important apprenticeship occurred under a Hawaiian tattoo artist. A one-hundred-year-old Polynesian woman who was famous for being a rebel within the world of art and feminism.

Each day with this tattoo artist felt new. Your other self loved grinding ink from kukui soot. She felt entranced by the tattoo artists' chants and dances by the fire. Even the long silences where they didn't talk for hours felt soothing to her soul.

This taught your other self how to be free. How to continuously release herself from all the rules, doubts, and fear that previously controlled her life. She unleashed her true potential.

She discovered the extent of her powers when she fell into a relationship with a struggling writer. He was about to give up writing his first novel, as he could not figure out how to turn his drab, lifeless writing into something special.

But your other self had a powerful effect on him. Together, they ran through the fields barefoot. She encouraged him to dance in public, even when there wasn't any music. She was beautiful. She was magnetic. Through her, he finally understood true creativity.

Your other self began to realize an undeniable truth. The universe had given her something precious, and she had to share it with the world.

At first, she started writing a blog. Through it, she shared her daily adventures with the world. She let her readers know how liberating it felt to be open to the universe.

To her surprise, her blog quickly became a hit. People from all over the world were fascinated by how carefree she lived. How she wasn't scared to try something new each day. Like performing jazz poetry at coffee shops. And officiating weddings on top of a mountain.

Through her blog, she received hundreds of messages. People from all around the world wrote to her about how lost and discouraged they felt. How nothing in life seemed to be working out for them.

She suddenly realized something profound. She had to craft a book to teach others what the universe had taught her.

But this wouldn't be just any self-help book. No, she dared to write a new kind of book. One that no one had ever seen before. It would unleash their inner free spirit. Fill their lives with hope and joy.

The book came to her in a series of dreams. She wrote with no plans, no outline. Just pure feeling and expression.

Suddenly, a downpour of inspiration came crashing into her. It summoned all the joy, wonder, and creativity she had experienced over the years. All the wisdom she had gleaned ever since she left her home and all its rules behind.

Her vision was powerful. Grand. Majestic. It awakened every ounce of her soul.

After it was finally done, she set out to share this miraculous story with the world. However, the world, with all its gatekeepers, didn't understand her vision.

Anytime she met with a publisher, they openly laughed at her work, pointing out all the ways she didn't follow the rules. They insinuated she was a delusional amateur writer. They treated her book, her entire life's work, like it was trash.

For a moment, she felt doubt. But then she remembered something the Hawaiian tattoo artist had told her about the nature of creativity. She said, "Never let the world hold you back. Be free. Dare to break the rules."

So she did. She refused to back down. She refused to give up on her creative vision.

She sold her car and all her possessions, using that money to fund the production of her book. Then, with an open heart, adventurous spirit, and rolling suitcase filled with books, she trekked across the country by bus and by foot.

At each stop, she did something that had never been done before: she gave the books to people for free. She gave her books to strangers in pubs. To mothers walking in the park. Even to college kids studying in cafes.

They could have tossed her book in the trash. Completely disregarded her and her book.

But miraculously, they read it. Devoured each and every page. They loved it. It left them in tears of joy.

They proudly placed the book on their nightstands.

For the book made them feel bold. It made them want to try new things in life. It made them feel absolutely free.

Soon, her book caught like wildfire. It appealed to everyone. Corporate workers, mothers, college students, waiters, teachers—everyone who had a dream. A dream to be who they truly were, not what society told them they had to be.

As your other self walked out into the world, people everywhere smiled at her. Cried as they shook her hand. Hugged her, and told her, "Thank you for everything you have done. Thank you for changing my life. I'm happy now because of you."

Years afterward, she reflected upon her grand journey. She felt honestly astonished by how far she had come. How she had started out as an ordinary girl who followed the rules. And ended up becoming a mentor to the entire world.

It was funny how all this happened. All because she wanted to know what it was like to be free.

※ ※ ※

This is your other self. She demonstrates your full potential.

You have heard her story. What part resonates most within you? What does it make you want to do?

If you look into your heart, you can see what you truly want. You want to break free. You yearn to feel alive.

In fact, you have always felt this intense yearning for freedom. You have always longed to live life your way, according to your own rules.

But why haven't you acted upon it? What is stopping you?

The answer can be found in the story of your other self. Like many people, she was raised to believe there was only one way to live. And she had to follow that one path, even if it made her unhappy. Even if it made her feel like she was dying inside.

But then your other self realized an important truth: *she didn't have to obey.*

Society tried to make her believe that she didn't have a choice. It told her that if she didn't follow the rules, she would be a horrible failure.

However, your other self dared to trust in the universe. She literally tore up the rules governing her life, and she went out alone into the unknown world.

It was an act of utter courage and faith. And in response, she attracted an inflection point. A moment in which the universe itself aligned, and it saw and recognized her—drawn to her wild, free-spirited nature and bold willingness to reimagine what living meant.

You can also make this choice. You can also choose to have faith in the universe and chase your dreams.

Thankfully, you have your alternate selves to show you the way. They can teach you how to break society's boundaries and reclaim your freedom. Such boldness and audacity will inevitably draw inflection points to you, like moths to a flame.

At this moment, visualize your Free-Spirited Self. She strides toward you, with wildflowers in her hair and a wide smile on her face. You notice the pure mischievousness in her eyes. The way she is always ready to laugh at the world.

Hear her speak:

I can see into your heart. It beats with an unquenchable thirst for adventure. It calls out to you, urging you to embark on a journey to explore the magnificent wonders of this vast universe.

Within you burns an intense longing—a powerful desire to fill your days with excitement, passion, and unbridled joy.

You need to let this yearning guide you. Don't let anyone tell you that you can't have an extraordinary life.

The truth is you are meant for something better. You are not supposed to be ordinary. You are not supposed to spend your days just quietly enduring life.

No, you will begin living the life you always wanted. And it starts right now.

Fortunately, you possess one instinct that will show you the way: your sense of fun and adventure.

Throughout your life, you have been taught that the right course of action is always dull and painful. That life is a matter of suffering rather than joy.

But what kind of life is that? You are a human being, not a machine. You are supposed to enjoy life. You are supposed to greet each day with a laugh and a smile.

So break free. Dare to break your usual routine. Start small if you must, but start today. Let spontaneity be your teacher. Replace "I should" with "I wonder." Trade caution for curiosity. Watch how the universe responds when you approach it with open arms rather than crossed arms.

Once you start doing this, you will find the universe answering you. When you start having fun, the universe will send you more opportunities for adventures.

And you will find that this will help unleash your destiny. Once you stop seeing life as a matter of painful work and obligation, then you will start seeing completely new possibilities. You will unlock your creativity on an unprecedented level.

So listen to your heart and to your yearning. They are trying to tell you something. They are showing you how to break free.

You are about to embark on the most exciting chapters of your life. As you open yourself to the universe, you will discover that you do have a destiny, one that leads to breathtaking adventure and freedom. Years from now, you will look back and realize that this was the first step of your grand journey.

Chapter 8

The Extraordinary Self

YOU FIND YOURSELF IN A MYSTERIOUS WAITING ROOM. IT IS BOTH minimalist and sexy. An elegant escape from the outside world.

The jazz and dreamy pop music fills the air as you observe the whimsical Parisian art installations next to you.

You have no idea why you are here or what's about to happen.

But from overhearing conversations of the people waiting next to you, you can tell you are in for a mind-blowing experience.

One man cannot contain his excitement. He has been on a five-year waiting list for this experience. Another woman took a ten-hour flight just to come here. This place has been on her bucket list for years.

As you watch people come out from behind a black curtain, they are buzzing with pure joy. Talking about how they never want to leave this place. How they are forever hooked. One person proclaimed, hands down, this was the best experience of his life.

Finally, it is your turn to enter through the black curtain. Your turn to find out what exactly makes this place so exceptional.

You are then seated at a table, in front of a covered dish. When the cover is removed, though, it suddenly feels extremely anticlimactic. All you see is a bowl of soup.

You think, *A bowl of soup? What can be so special about soup? People wait five years for this?*

But when you taste the soup, you get emotional. You feel as if you have been transported back to your childhood. Back to a simpler time when your mother spent all Sunday making soup for you. Putting her love and care into it.

You will dream about this soup for a long time.

After you finish your twelve-course Kaiseki meal, you leave the restaurant, thinking your day can't get any better than this.

But as you exit through the doors, you notice you are right in the middle of the Las Vegas Strip. Above you, you see a massive, glittering video billboard of a confident-looking chef. Her eyes look fierce, as if she knows she's the best.

You realize this must be her restaurant.

But when you look more closely at the billboard, you suddenly notice that it is your face. For in this universe, your alternate self is an icon in the food world. Her talent as a chef led her to a global empire of acclaimed restaurants as well as hosting the most popular cooking TV shows.

However, your alternate self didn't start out this successful. Actually, for most of her life, she felt the complete opposite. She used to believe that great things in life could never happen to someone like her.

Your alternate self grew up feeling inadequate. She thought she wasn't the prettiest. Wasn't the smartest. Didn't have any particular talents. Because she couldn't see anything good about herself, she felt so small and plain.

She thought that by going to college, she could maybe find her purpose there. But college felt like an overwhelming jungle.

Without any direction in life, she changed her majors many times. Nothing felt right. Nothing "clicked."

Feeling so lost and ashamed after graduation, she applied to many jobs but got almost none of them. The only job she got was a sales job for a paper company.

While working at her job every day, she had to answer calls about paper. Deal with rude clients. Talk about a product she cared nothing for.

It was a soul-sucking job.

She thought that she would only stay at this job for a few months. That at some point, she'd find something better. But those few months turned into a few years. Ten, to be exact.

Her family nagged at her constantly, wondering why she was still at the same dead-end job for such a long time. They asked her why she couldn't get a better job. What about grad school? A husband? Kids?

Everyone made her feel like a failure for having none of those things. And when she turned thirty-five, she wondered if she would always feel this stuck. If she was doomed to live a mediocre, unfulfilled life.

But little did she know, her fate would change one night.

It was during one of the many nights in which she tried to watch TV to fall asleep. Hoping any show could take her mind off her incessant worrying about her dire future.

As she was scrolling through the channels, though, your other self was mesmerized by the host of one cooking TV show. The chef was a warm and charming Southern woman who could whip up all kinds of magic in the kitchen. She could turn humble, everyday ingredients into breathtaking Michelin-star meals.

The chef closed each show with a warm smile and famous catchphrase: "Remember, with cooking, the ordinary can become the extraordinary."

Your other self suddenly teared up at that moment. It felt like the TV chef was talking directly to her. Telling her that she had a bright future. That it wasn't too late. That, through cooking, she could turn her ordinary life into something extraordinary.

But at the same time, she was also filled with doubt. She was already thirty-five, and she knew nothing about cooking.

What made her think she could actually do this? What if she was really bad at it? What if changing careers was a huge mistake?

However, she could not deny the fact that cooking was the only thing that made her smile. The only thing that made her life worth living.

She could not sleep that night. She was suddenly aware of a truth she had long suppressed: she had to do something with her life. For as long as she could remember, she had waited. Waited for something to happen. Waited for her life to begin.

But no more. She felt a sudden wild urge to seize life. She was done with waiting.

It was at that moment that your other self attracted an inflection point.

Later on, she struggled to describe this moment to others. How the ordinary fluorescent light of her apartment glowed brighter than ever, as if it suddenly sprang alive. How the silence itself deepened as if the world stood still for her. As if the universe held its breath, waiting to see what she would do next.

At that moment, your other self manifested her greatest desire: *to be the best chef in the entire world.*

Everything felt different to her now. That night, she stayed up exploring her kitchen, as if it was a completely new place. Tasting every spice. Smelling every herb. Like a magician, she tried to figure out what tasted good with what.

She hadn't felt this excited about her life in a long time.

Every day after work, she looked forward to practicing her

cooking. Her favorite thing to do was to get lost in the grocery store aisles, transfixed by the number of Southeast Asian sauces and Oaxacan dried chiles.

She wanted to taste everything. Cook everything. Discover everything there was to know about food. Learn how to turn the ordinary into the extraordinary.

The more she studied cooking, the deeper she fell into her passion. She became so serious about becoming a chef that she decided to take a huge risk.

Your other self abruptly quit her job at the paper company. Using all her savings, she booked a one-way ticket to France and enrolled in cooking school there.

Everyone was so shocked by what your other self did. She normally lived her life in a very safe and predictable way. Never before had she done anything so bold.

However, she knew life was short, and she didn't want to spend another day waiting for her life to begin. She wanted to start living *now*.

When your other self arrived in Paris, she immediately fell in love with the city. Every morning, she woke up to the smell of freshly baked croissants and sipped on cappuccino that made her do a happy dance on the cobblestone floor. As she nibbled on the brie she tried from each cheese store, she thought, W*ow, I really belong here.*

But on her first day of cooking school, she felt extremely out of place. Everyone in her class seemed so young, barely twenty. They bragged to one another of the restaurants they had already worked at. And here she was, a thirty-five-year-old, clearly the oldest person in the class. The only one with no professional experience.

She felt absolutely sure she would fail. If everyone else was already so far ahead in their culinary career, how could she ever catch up and be on their level?

At the end of the week, all the students lined up in a straight line, military style, ready to present their bowl of bouillabaisse, a tomato seafood soup.

The head instructor had no smile as he tasted each soup. He publicly berated a student for their unrefined knife skills. He spat out soup when it was far below his standards.

When he came to try your other self's soup, though, he closed his eyes and was silent for a while. Your other self figured she must have the worst soup in the entire class.

But the instructor let out a small smile. He looked straight into your other self's eyes and said, "You were born to cook."

Everyone else in the class tried her soup and was blown away by how good it tasted. The instructor explained to the class that *this* was what real cooking was. Taking your memories, your soul, and folding that into your food, one layer at a time.

Your other self was at a loss for words. The entire time she thought she was at a disadvantage. She assumed she was behind in life. That she had nothing of value to offer to the world.

But she was beginning to realize what she did have. All those decades of yearning had sharpened her awareness. Made her more sensitive to emotions. And this became her greatest advantage.

Now she could feel deeply. Now she knew what people most longed for: to feel alive.

And because she knew all these things, because of her own personal experiences, she could use food to connect with people. To tap into their desire for adventure. Their desire to dream, to savor each and every moment of life.

After graduating from culinary school, she was very eager to bring her food vision to life. However, she knew she had to first gain experience working at restaurants. Which meant she needed to start at the very bottom as a prep cook.

Most people wouldn't do what your other self did. They

wouldn't start a new career at the age of thirty-five. Earn less money. Work longer hours. Wake up at four every morning to cut vegetables for hours.

But your other self had never felt more alive. While she was stirring soup, she could feel herself creating art. Creating that first bite, that first impression that would wow the customers.

None of this felt like work because she was living her dream.

Customers kept coming back for her soup, and soon, your other self's cooking was in high demand. She continued to turn heads by beautifully mastering each station in the kitchen. Her boss was so impressed by her cooking that she was eventually promoted to sous chef.

Offers began pouring in from other restaurants that begged her to cook for them. Your other self could not believe what was happening to her. Not too long ago, she was just some unknown person at a dead-end job. Now she had her pick of the best chef positions in town.

Your other self worked at other high-end restaurants and started to create a name for herself, becoming somewhat of a local star. People waited months, sometimes even a year to eat at her restaurants. Magazine articles, TV segments, and countless vlogs covered her food, dubbing her the "hottest rising chef."

While your other self loved her new life as a chef, she still had the burning desire to do more. She had spent years cooking other people's culinary visions, which truly helped her develop as a chef. But her dream was to open up a restaurant of her own. Cook her own style of food. Truly express the breadth of her life experiences through her cuisine.

So she penny pinched and saved every day to help fund the opening of her new restaurant. Investors also loved her restaurant concept, a whimsical take on a French bistro, which was her love letter to Paris.

The best moment was seeing her entire restaurant come together.

It was all beautifully planned out. She would have jazz nights at the restaurant every Friday. A cozy cobblestone patio where people could enjoy their cappuccinos. Intimate candlelit areas that marked that perfect date night. As she wrote all her dinner specials on the black chalkboard, she couldn't stop smiling.

She finally did it. She finally achieved her dream. She was so proud of how she restarted her life. How she started from the bottom and reached the top. It felt like nothing could ruin this perfect moment.

But a few days before her restaurant was set to open, an unexpected yet deadly pandemic swept the world. In an attempt to protect its people from this unknown airborne virus, governments mandated that everyone quarantine in their own homes.

These were truly unprecedented times. Schools around the world abruptly closed. Entire economies crashed overnight. Restaurants everywhere were forced to shut down, as the virus made it too dangerous for people to be physically near each other.

It was all out of her hands. Your other self could not open her new restaurant. Unable to make a profit, she had no choice but to close her bistro.

It was a series of bad events. She lost all the money she put into the restaurant. She had to let go of all her staff. She was in so much debt from all the restaurant renovations that she even had to sell her car.

Your other self was beyond devastated. It was as if her entire world, the future she had worked so hard for, had crumbled overnight.

But somehow, she didn't let this destroy her. She found the strength to keep going, knowing that she had already been through worse times.

She thought back to how powerless she had felt in her old life. When she had worked at her meaningless desk job. And had no dreams.

And tears came to her eyes when she thought about that cooking TV show that saved her life. It showed her that there was another way to live. That it was never too late to achieve greatness.

Cooking had saved her then, and cooking would save her now. Nothing, not even a pandemic, could stop her from cooking with love.

Your other self was determined to find other ways to bring her food to the people. She started to post social media videos of herself making her famous soup and other dishes.

While she cooked, she didn't merely recite the steps to her dish. She also told many personal stories. Some were jokes about how awkward it was to date during the pandemic. Others were inspiring stories of how she quit her desk job to chase a dream.

These were simple stories, but they reminded viewers of their shared, beautiful humanity. A humanity that was strong enough to conquer anything, even a global pandemic.

As a result, your other self was the light that people needed in these dark times. When people cooked her recipes, they felt connected to her stories and her soul. When they tasted her food, they cried, thinking of their childhood, of their dreams, of how the pandemic was the best time to reinvent themselves.

After the pandemic ended, your other self found tremendous success. She built a food empire of restaurants all over the world. She became the face of the culinary world, elevating food like no one had ever done before.

One dish at a time, her food liberated people. It set them free from their preconceived notions of how life was supposed to be. It showed them that it was never too late to turn their lives around.

That even the ordinary can become the extraordinary.

Millions of people followed in your other self's footsteps. Her food and story inspired them to do bold things they had never done before. They gained the courage to quit their meaningless jobs. And chase their dreams.

People weren't afraid to start over. To become beginners in new fields. To get out of their comfort zone. To regard their future as an exciting adventure rather than see it as a boring chore.

This was your other self's legacy. And her food, her art, forever changed the way people lived, loved, and dreamed.

***

This is your other self. She demonstrates your full potential.

What could happen once you find your passion? The one thing that would make you feel alive? The one pursuit that would give you a sense of meaning and purpose?

Then everything in life would click. You would wake up each day feeling refreshed and eager. You would achieve at unimaginable levels. You would lead a thrilling life of adventure.

This is exactly what happened to your Extraordinary Self. Before she discovered her passion, she was an unhappy paper salesperson. To the outside world, she appeared utterly ordinary. Someone destined to lead an uninteresting life.

But everything changed once she discovered her passion. Then she began wandering through exotic marketplaces, searching for intoxicating new flavor combinations. She even dared to start a brand new life in France.

You can do the same. You can also find your purpose.

As Mark Twain famously declared, "The two most important days in your life are the day you are born and the day you find out why."

The truth is that you are on this planet for a reason. Your job is to discover what that reason is.

You might have already spent time searching. You might have already attempted several possible careers.

However, there is one thing that you haven't done. One thing that will open completely new possibilities that you have never imagined.

This is what you have yet to do: *purposefully go the wrong way.*

This may sound like strange advice. After all, you are trying to find the right path to your dreams. The last thing you want to do is waste time going in the wrong direction.

However, you have to remember this absolute truth: the universe is vast and mysterious.

It is far larger than our conception of it. We think that we see all our possible choices. We think that we know what will happen.

But we are wrong. The universe has countless surprises waiting for us. Surprises that are beautiful and breathtaking.

And the best way to find these surprises is to go the wrong direction.

It makes complete sense that we are more likely to attract inflection points when we go down the wrong path. When we consciously trust in the universe—when we become open to the universe's bounty—we are rewarded.

For example, in the story of your Extraordinary Self, you will remember that everyone thought she was making a mistake when she wanted to become a chef. At the time, she was in her thirties, with no professional cooking experience. It seemed folly for her to give up her safe job to pursue a quixotic dream of cooking in France.

Yet she did it anyway. She embraced the foolish, absurd, and impossible. She went against everyone's advice and warnings.

And the universe rewarded her for such nerve and audacity. It gave her a dream life that she never thought possible.

The universe is also waiting for you. It is waiting for you to embrace the unknown. To go beyond the familiar and expected.

And you can do it, especially with the assistance of your alternate selves.

At this moment, visualize your Extraordinary Self. See her bright eyes watching you with an expression of utter joy and delight. She laughs and spins in front of you, saying:

> You may envy me. I have done and seen things that I never thought possible.
>
> But in truth, I am envious of you. You are about to experience one of the greatest moments of your life. You are about to realize a truth that will set you free.
>
> This is the truth: you exist in a world far larger than you ever imagined.
>
> For most of my early life, I thought that the world was a small place. I thought that there was nothing more to the world than my cubicle and my dull, everyday life.
>
> But I was so wrong. The universe has so many wonders and surprises. You just have to look in unexpected places to find these treasures.
>
> And this is what you are going to do. You are going to wander off the beaten path. You are going to purposefully lose yourself. You are going to go in unexpected directions.
>
> Because you have to get lost before you can be found.

You were never supposed to lead an ordinary life of routine. You are the descendant of explorers and pioneers. You are meant to search for the new and unexpected.

You are supposed to do things that surprise even you. Life is supposed to be an astonishing adventure.

The reason that you have yet to find your passion is that you were only looking in expected places. In only the few areas that society told you to look.

But that is not the life that you want or need. You are meant to dare things that you didn't think possible.

Because that is where your passion is. It will be in the most surprising of places. And it will be better than you had ever thought possible.

And I will accompany you on this amazing journey. I will be there to remind you that mistakes are okay. That you are supposed to wander. That you can embrace the spontaneous.

And when you get to your destination, you will finally understand the meaning of your life.

And all this starts with the decision to go the wrong way. The choice to trust in the universe. To believe that you have a destiny to go beyond the known and familiar.

You feel a deep part of your soul respond to her words. You realize that this is what you have always yearned for. A life beyond the ordinary. A thrilling life that contains unexpected chapters and rewards. *Your life.*

Chapter 9

The Irresistible Self

YOU STEP INTO AN APARTMENT HALLWAY THAT FEELS LIKE IT was built from your memories.

The details are perfect—too perfect. Like someone reached into your mind and constructed this place from all the past apartments you used to live in but got everything slightly, magnificently wrong. The light is softer here. The shadows fall differently, and the air itself feels like it's holding its breath.

Then, a booming sound hits you like a kiss from a thunderstorm. Your first instinct is to laugh. Someone is throwing the kind of college party that would've gotten you evicted from every apartment you've ever had.

But wait.

Something's different about tonight's impromptu concert. The sound isn't just loud—it's alive. Electric. It wraps around you like a current, making every nerve ending dance.

You're enchanted. Because underneath that earth-shaking bass, there's a voice that makes your heart skip a beat.

You've heard this voice before. In your shower, when you think no one's listening. In your car, during those long midnight drives. In those dreams where you're brave enough to sing what you really feel.

Drawn toward the music like a moth to a dangerous flame, you round the corner and notice something odd—an apartment door is wide open, spilling light into the hallway. The kind of light that belongs in music videos and fever dreams.

You step closer, and your world splits wide open.

Every wall of this apartment is covered in floor-to-ceiling TV screens, all playing the same footage: Madison Square Garden, packed beyond capacity. But it's the woman on stage who makes your breath catch in your throat.

This woman is wearing a dress that seems to be made of broken mirrors and bad intentions. Every movement catches light like a supernova. Her hair is wild, untamed, exactly how yours looks in the morning—except somehow she's turned that chaos into a crown. When she struts across the stage, the camera zooms in on her boots: combat boots covered in glitter and what look like actual stars.

The music she's playing isn't just breaking records—it's breaking rules. It's Taylor Swift's songwriting genius cranked up to eleven, mixed with Lady Gaga's fearlessness and a dash of something entirely new.

She grabs the mic stand like she's claiming a kingdom. She launches into a song about burning down expectations and building castles from the ashes. It's the kind of song that would make your mother blush and your ex-boyfriends nervous. The kind of song that feels like a beautiful crime.

On the screens, the crowd goes completely wild. You notice that there are over one hundred thousand people. And they are all shouting the same name over and over again.

When you get a better look at the woman rocking out on stage, you suddenly realize she has the same face as yours, but with some crucial differences.

Her smile belongs in a museum of dangerous things. She's got your eyes, but they're lined with something that makes them look like weapons. Your lips, but painted in a shade that should come with a warning label. Even your nervous habit of biting your lower lip has been transformed into something that makes the front row swoon.

The headline ticker at the bottom of the TV screen reads: Biggest Tour in History Continues to Break Records: Controversial Queen of Music Sells Out Global Stadium Tour in Three Minutes.

This is your alternate self. In this universe, she is the greatest rock star of all time. Every song she releases becomes a generation's anthem, every performance a religious experience. She turns stadiums into temples and critics into believers. The world isn't just obsessed with her music—they're addicted to her audacity, her divine defiance, her ability to make chaos look like courage.

But here's the plot twist that makes her legend even more intoxicating: fifteen years ago, your alternate self believed her existence was a mistake. She used to apologize for taking up space in the world. In high school, she was clearly unpopular, but she never quite understood why.

She spent hours in front of her mirror at night, analyzing every detail of her reflection like a crime scene. Was it the way she laughed? How she walked? The clothes she wore? Or something deeper? Some fundamental flaw that everyone could see but her?

All she knew was whenever she entered a room, people suddenly acted awkward and bored. At parties—the few times she was accidentally invited—she became furniture, less noticeable than the potted plants. She measured her worth in negative spaces: the empty chairs beside her in class, the group conversations that died whenever she joined them, the text messages that remained unread.

The other girls called her Charity Case. Not even to be mean—they'd just forgotten her real name. The boys made bets about asking her out as a joke. She kept a diary full of crossed-out dreams and tearstained pages, each entry starting with "Why am I like this?"

She was the protagonist of no one's story—not even her own.

However, one day, her life was changed when she saw a music video.

It started innocently enough on her laptop screen at three in the morning—one of those nights when loneliness felt like a physical weight. Just another music video: an ordinary girl walking down an ordinary street. The kind of girl who apologizes when someone else bumps into her. The kind of girl who hates her mirror reflection every day.

But then—revolution.

The transformation wasn't just physical; it was atomic. The girl in the video didn't just become beautiful—she became nuclear. Her eyes held galaxies. Her smile could make emperors surrender their crowns. But it was her attitude. God, her attitude. The way she wore confidence like it had been invented just for her.

Your alternate self couldn't breathe. Couldn't move. Couldn't look away. For years, she'd believed that girls like her could never be beautiful. That she was born to be a background character in someone else's story.

But this video screamed a truth she'd been too afraid to touch: that maybe invisibility was a choice. That maybe all those quiet girls reading poetry in bathroom stalls were secretly queens plotting to turn the kingdom upside down.

With her hands shaking, she turned to her mirror—that old enemy that had cataloged her flaws for so many years. But tonight, something electric happened. Instead of counting imperfections, she saw possibility. Raw, wild, beautiful possibility.

She flipped her hair—not the careful way they taught in magazines, but like she was trying to start a hurricane. She wore a smile that turned good girls bad and bad girls legendary. She grabbed her hairbrush like it was a microphone, and for the first time in her life, she didn't apologize for the space she took up.

The universe held its breath.

In that moment, something fundamental shifted. Like reality itself had been waiting for her to finally catch fire. She could feel it in her bones—the girl who apologized for existing was gone. In her place stood someone who made rebellion look like art, someone who could turn her scars into songs and her fears into fire.

Her voice came out like thunder breaking chains: "I'm going to become the world's greatest rock star."

The universe noticed. Of course it did. How could it ignore a girl who had finally learned to speak in lightning? Her newfound boldness even allowed her to do a history project in the style of K-pop rap.

Classmates didn't just notice—they were absolutely bewitched. That magnetic shift from invisible to inevitable turned their world upside down. The same people who once looked through her now couldn't remember how to breathe when she entered a room.

After her class performance, she smiled to herself, realizing that sometimes the quietest girls made the loudest revolutions.

But not everyone was ready for her transformation. Her parents thought she was delusional for trying to be a singer. They constantly warned her of all the bad things that could happen to her. They made her feel like she was crazy to chase her dreams.

Without any support from her parents, she decided to pursue singing on her own. She worked at several restaurants so she could move out into the city and pay for singing lessons.

Some nights, at the restaurant, she wiped the outdoor tables and sang to herself, belting out tunes when she thought no one was watching.

The manager once caught her singing and was intrigued by the unique sound of her voice. He then offered her an opportunity to sing a few nights per week at the restaurant.

But when she sang at the restaurant during her first few months, most of her audience ignored her. Throughout her performances, all she could hear were the sounds of forks scraping plates.

No one was paying attention to her. No one knew she was even there. It felt like high school all over again.

But your other self didn't give up. She kept performing at the restaurant. Doing everything she could to hone her craft. Trying to embody the attitude she loved from that music video.

Eventually, she got better and better. She felt more comfortable with the audience and could interact with them. Flirt with them. Be sassy with them. Lose herself to the soulfulness of the music.

Soon, more and more people came to the restaurant just to listen to her. They were mesmerized by her performances. She even got the attention of a studio executive who wanted to give her a record deal on the spot.

No one had ever said yes to her. Yes to her talent. Yes to her potential. She never thought something like this could ever happen to her.

Suddenly, her life changed overnight. She went from waiting tables to recording songs at the studio.

She woke up early every morning to get glammed up by her hair and makeup team. Then, she flew all over the country to promote her music at malls, food festivals, and outdoor concerts.

She loved performing on stage. It made her feel alive. It made her feel powerful.

Her popularity exploded over the next few months. It seemed like a party followed her everywhere she went. Girls started screaming every time they saw your other self. Whenever she strutted into the room with her studded boots and her sultry laugh, she drove men absolutely crazy.

While her music career looked perfect on the outside, your other self felt miserable on the inside. After she signed her music contract, the record company took complete control of her career.

They tried to make her over so she conformed to one standard of beauty. Made her lips full and clothes skin tight. Changed her hair and makeup so she fulfilled men's fantasies.

As each day passed, she felt increasing pressure to become someone she wasn't. An artificial bubblegum-pop idol. An agreeable girl who smiled all the time and caused no trouble.

She started to lose her true identity. She missed the girl she used to be. The fiery girl who dared to become the world's greatest rock star. The uninhibited waitress who sang soulfully at the restaurant.

Your other self made the fateful decision to no longer be the record label's puppet. She chose to defy them and do music her own way.

Weeks prior to her concert, she changed all the costumes. She fired her dance choreographer. She even changed the set list and included songs that the record label had already rejected.

Her manager and her entire team were shocked by her risky behavior. They warned her not to be so bold. Not to go against the record label. Not to jeopardize her career like this.

When the music executives found out what your other self was doing, they immediately dropped her from the label. Since she was unwilling to follow the traditional ways musicians should look and perform, they believed she could never make it in this industry.

For a while, your other self thought her career was over. She feared she had overstepped her boundaries. She wondered if she should have been more cooperative. Less outspoken.

But amid the turmoil in her career, one moment kept tugging at her heart. It was the moment when she watched that music video as a young girl. When she discovered that beauty came from embracing your true self.

Your other self embarked on a journey to reinvent herself as a musician. She threw away all the costumes and old ways of the record label. And she moved back home to her childhood bedroom to reconnect to the best parts of herself.

Everyone was confused by what she was doing. She seemed to suddenly disappear from the limelight.

Rumors began to spread about your other self. How she was quietly going through a mental breakdown. How she was in denial of her failure. Some people even seemed excited to see her crash and burn with her new record.

But they were all wrong about her. She was not lost.

She was not afraid. In fact, she felt in charge of her life. She hadn't felt this way in a long time.

Using what savings she had left, she produced her own concert. Without the constraints of her old record label, she could do music completely her own way. Embrace authenticity rather than superficiality.

Preparing for the concert on her own was one of the hardest things she had ever done. She had to constantly fight back thoughts of failure. Thoughts of people not believing in her vision. The idea of fans not liking her new music.

But when she finally took the stage, she mustered up the courage to do her own thing. She wore no makeup. No high heels. No fancy sets. The stage was completely bare except for her and her acoustic guitar.

At first, this seemed like a complete disaster. The audience held their breath, waiting for a terrible concert to unfold.

But then she began to sing. She sank to her knees, pouring

her soul into each song. Expressing the need to be herself and no one else.

The stadium grew quiet as the audience clung to every word and note. Never before had they witnessed something so pure. So raw. So powerful.

Suddenly, thousands of women realized something profound. Something they were not supposed to say out loud or feel in their hearts.

They realized how beautiful they were when they were just being themselves. And this epiphany made them break down in tears.

But these were happy tears. Tears of utter freedom and joy. The entire audience cheered your other self on as she tore the stage up with her raw, uncensored music.

Magic was in the air that night. Girls were dancing and singing their hearts out. No other performance had ever made them feel this good. Never before had they felt this alive.

Her music swept the entire world, becoming the soundtrack of people's lives. As people rode the subways, brushed their teeth, or went for their morning run, they played her music. And it transported them into another world.

A world where anything was possible. Where the least popular girl could instantly feel sexy. Where lonely girls felt heard and seen. Where the quiet girls surprised everyone and defied the rules.

Her music forever changed society. The idea that beauty had to be a certain way—a harrowing dress size and an unrealistic Facetuned look? Your other self shattered those toxic standards with her songs.

People everywhere changed the way they lived their lives. They used to worry about not fitting in or not being liked. They used to believe that they couldn't be happy without society's approval of them.

But after listening to your other self's music, millions of fans made the bold decision to throw all those old rules out the window. Your other self being so bold and unapologetic made people tap into an inner sexiness they didn't know they had.

Soon, this universe became a happier place for many people. Her music helped them realize that life is not worth living if you cannot be who you are. Especially when the real you is beautiful beyond comprehension.

✯ ✯ ✯

This is your other self. She demonstrates your full potential.

Here is the key question: what makes someone irresistible?

You might think that it is just a matter of physical appearance. Perfect skin, a button nose, and voluptuous lips. That only someone with this specific look can ever be irresistible.

However, we know that is not true. Cleopatra was not the most conventionally beautiful woman in ancient Egypt. Contemporary accounts mention that her nose was too large and her lips too thin.

Yet everyone agrees that she was absolutely irresistible. Her confident charm and spunk mesmerized everyone in her kingdom. She was so enthralling that Roman emperors begged for a chance to be by her side. Someone so desirable that wars were fought for her sake.

And in our own lives, we know plenty of individuals who simply have that "it" factor. They may not be the most conventionally beautiful people, but they clearly have something special. Something that draws the eye, quickens the heart, and makes you remember them long afterward.

The truth is that anyone is capable of becoming this irresistible. So how?

When you look back upon the life of your Irresistible Self, you will notice the key moment when everything changed. It occurred when she was young and she dared to declare her greatest dream: "One day, I'm going to become the world's greatest rock star."

Note that she didn't state that she was going to try to be a successful singer. Nor did she say that she was going to get music lessons and see what happened.

Instead, she had the audacity to proclaim that she was going to be the world's greatest rock star. Such confidence is sexy. Such boldness is irresistible.

If you know that you are daring and sexy, others can feel that confidence. The more you believe in your irresistibility, the more they will believe in it as well.

Your perception of yourself is that powerful. It is like a huge signal flare to the universe, proclaiming your true value and worth. It will attract inflection points like moths to a flame.

And you are capable of such bold confidence. You have it within you to be this irresistible to the entire world.

However, this is difficult because you have to go against everything you have been taught. You have to see the world and yourself in completely new ways.

Instead of following the conventional notion of beauty, you must redefine it yourself. Just as Cleopatra did.

Fortunately, you have alternate selves who can show you how to bring out such extraordinary boldness.

Right now, picture your Irresistible Self. In your mind's eye, what do you notice first? Is it her hair? Her clothes?

You will note that what looms largest is her vibe. Watch how she struts toward you. Each bold step seems to declare, "This is who I am. Look how sexy I am. With each step, I challenge the entire world."

And when she stands before you, you can literally feel her charisma. You find yourself wanting to be in her presence. Just to feel her breathtaking energy.

You meet her electric, knowing gaze. You can feel her coolly appraising you. Seeing deep into your very soul.

She speaks to you:

I am going to tell you something that will blow your mind.

What if everything you know about beauty is a carefully constructed lie? What if the magazines, the influencers, the billion-dollar industries are all selling you smoke and mirrors?

True beauty is an act of rebellion. It's the audacity to look the world in the eye and refuse to shrink yourself to fit inside its tiny boxes. While others whisper, you'll roar. While they follow, you'll forge your own path through the wilderness.

Here's the dangerous truth they don't want you to know: you are already a force of nature. You are lightning bottled in human form. The only cage holding back your magnificence is the one you've built yourself.

Stop asking for permission to be extraordinary. Your fire isn't meant to warm others—it's meant to ignite revolutions. The world doesn't need another perfectly polished reflection. It needs your glorious, untamed spirit set free.

So this is your mission. Throw out all that society has taught you. Throw away all your preconceptions of what true beauty is.

Never let anyone tone down your inner sexiness.

And when you openly and unapologetically defy society like this, you send a clear message to the universe. You declare, "This is who I am. I am worthy of tremendous love, respect, and success. I stand irresistible and undeniable to the world."

Deep inside you, you feel yourself respond to these words. You are aware of your inner fire and hunger. You are aware that you can stand this proudly and unapologetically. You are aware that you are irresistible and beautiful beyond words.

Chapter 10

The Positive Self

YOU ARE IN AN ALTERNATE WORLD. IT IS ONE COMPLETELY AT war. Everywhere you look, you see devastated cities. Mothers and children huddle in bomb shelters as their homes are destroyed by rockets and drones. Some regions have already begun to starve.

All hope seems to be lost as countries throughout the world succumb to dictators and tyrants. Humanity seems on the brink of utter self-destruction.

But then an image appears on every screen across the planet. It is a woman, beautiful and radiant. She glows with fierce hope and optimism. She declares to the world, as president of the United States, that she has put a stop to the warfare. That the free nations of the world have joined together to finally create a new world order. One defined by freedom, equality, and opportunity for everyone.

Everywhere, people applaud their savior. People emerge from bomb shelters with a newfound sense of hope. The air becomes electric with joy and happiness.

And it is only then that you recognize the woman on the screen. It is your face. She is your alternate self.

How did your other self reach the pinnacle of political success? By all rights, this should have been impossible. Because your other self grew up in a socially and economically devastated community. One in which there were almost no jobs. And most people had to survive on welfare. It was a bleak environment, marked by rampant crime and despair.

Early in her life, your other self gave in to the hopelessness of her surroundings. It was hard not to. Nearly everyone in her life was a dropout or alcoholic. She never even knew her father because he was in prison when she was born.

Once she was asked to write an essay describing her ideal future. The only thing she did was scrawl in thick black ink, "I have no future."

Like so many of her friends, she turned to petty crime, primarily shoplifting. And as she grew older, she joined gangs. She participated in organized crime sprees, brazenly stealing from shopping malls and warehouses. With each year, her crimes became worse.

And then one day she was caught and arrested by the police. The police officer who arrested her was a kind older man. He tried to speak to her, explaining that she could do so much with her life.

In response, she unleashed all her pent-up anger and despair. She screamed at him that she had no life. That she came from an environment in which no one had a chance. That everywhere she looked, she only saw dead ends and wasted lives.

The police officer stared at her and then asked her the question that would change her entire life: "Is that all you see?"

At that moment, your other self's mind suddenly opened. She abruptly realized that she was only seeing one version of reality. That the world was so much larger and grander than she had ever envisioned.

When she went home, she saw everything differently. She

noticed how hard the people of her community worked. She saw the teacher staying after school without pay in order to help the neediest students. She saw the baker who woke up early to open his store and stayed late to feed the homeless. She saw the single mother selling roses by the freeway.

Your other self saw all these things, and in that fateful moment, she made a decision. She resolved to lead her life differently. To be a source of comfort to her community, a light in their darkest hours.

Because of her bold and sudden choice, she attracted an inflection point. And she was able to manifest her greatest desire: to become the protector that her people needed.

The universe saw and heard her. And it granted her this wish.

Suddenly, her vision expanded even more. Now, she could see the world as it actually was—full of hope, beauty, and wonder. And this gave her unparalleled strength, a positivity that shone like the sun.

As soon as she graduated high school, she joined the police academy. There, even seasoned police officers felt themselves drawn to her pure vision and soul. It was not a surprise that, upon graduation, she was given the position that she desired: a beat officer patrolling the same streets where she had grown up.

In that position, she was able to perform miracles. She turned people's lives around with a word or even a gesture. Once, a fight broke out between rival gangs, but she resolved it by having a quiet meeting with the leaders. One of the leaders became so inspired by her words that he quit a life of crime.

Your other self quickly rose up the ranks of the police force. She became a detective, and she found that even hardened criminals responded to her radiant, positive energy. They gave her the clues that she needed to solve crimes that had long perplexed her colleagues. And then against all odds, she became captain of the entire police force, the first woman to do so.

In her promotion ceremony, she spoke vulnerably about what being a public servant meant to her. In a choked voice, she described the impact of the police officer she had met as an angry youth. A recording of her speech went viral and inspired thousands of at-risk youths to turn their lives around.

Soon people clamored for her to run for mayor. And she did so because she believed it was the path to helping the most people. However, her city was notorious for its corruption. In actuality, the true power lay in the hands of a small group of corrupt businessmen and politicians. They were the ones who decided who became mayor.

However, this group feared your other self's growing popularity. They didn't want her to run for mayor. To persuade her, they offered her millions of dollars. But she secretly recorded the bribe offer, thus exposing the businessmen and politicians. And with the resulting publicity, she became the first female mayor of her city.

In that role, your other self accomplished the extraordinary. She ended corruption. She was able to turn around her once-blighted community. Where there were once rows of boarded-up buildings and abandoned storefronts, there were now thriving small businesses and beautiful apartment complexes.

People couldn't get enough of her. They were all mesmerized by her dazzling positive energy. They asked her to run for senator. And she did, winning easily.

Then came your other self's greatest challenge. Several years earlier, a dictatorial president had seized control of America. He had sown division, turning everyone in the nation against each other. He had broadcast a message of hate and misogyny that had spread distrust and fear throughout the country. And everyone believed him to be absolutely unstoppable.

But your other self dared oppose him. She announced that she would run for president, and he immediately attacked her. His legions of followers dug into her past, seeking anything incriminating. They discovered that she had been a juvenile delinquent. That she had stolen merchandise from businesses throughout her community. That she had been a member of several gangs.

The president gleefully declared that she was unfit for public office. He crowed that she was a disgrace to her community and to America.

Suddenly, everything came crashing down for your other self. Her worst fears had come true. She had once believed in hope and redemption. But now everyone saw her as a criminal. Social media buzzed with condemnation for her past actions.

For a moment, your other self went to a dark place. She could not see a way forward, and she felt despair.

Then she remembered that long-ago moment with the police officer. He had asked her the most important question of her life: "Is that all you see?"

And your other self suddenly realized that she could see light where other people could only see darkness. She rallied herself and began to earnestly fight the president.

Polls showed that she was way behind, but she didn't care. She boldly attacked the president. She openly taunted him until he agreed to debate her in front of the entire world.

There, people could suddenly see the stark differences between the two candidates. He was cynical and dark. He believed that the world was a brutal place in which only the strong could survive.

In contrast, your other self shined with hope and positivity. She proclaimed that it was possible to create a world defined by equality, compassion, and opportunity for everyone.

Suddenly, everything changed. People began to realize they were collectively capable of grace, mercy, and courage. They treated each other with kindness and understanding. They remembered that they had once been a great nation and could be great again. It was as if your other self had unleashed the true noble spirit of the people.

A tidal wave of unstoppable support swept through the country. She soared up in the polls. And in the general elections, despite the president's fiercest and most desperate efforts, she utterly destroyed him, becoming the first female president of the United States. And the nation became whole once again.

Your other self healed her country just in time. As its leader, she went on to repair a fractured planet, ending a world war and launching a new era of unparalleled peace and prosperity in every country. She became the greatest leader her world had ever seen.

✯ ✯ ✯

This is your other self. She demonstrates your full potential.

You will notice that it took only five simple words to transform her life: "Is that all you see?"

For all of us, it is easy to only focus on certain parts of our lives. To only see the negatives. To only notice our failures and setbacks. To only perceive the barriers that stand in our way.

However, in doing so, we ignore larger truths. For example, your other self had an epiphany when she truly saw her community for the first time.

Before, she had only noticed poverty and crime. But then she perceived the courage, kindness, and hope that suffused her neighborhood. And it utterly transformed her understanding of the world.

Because of these insights, your other self was inspired to choose a different life for herself. And because of that choice, she attracted an inflection point—an opportunity to change her life in an instant.

You can also attract inflection points. You can also completely change your life.

It's probably clear to you what initiates many inflection points: a sudden opening of our mind. A realization that we have only been seeing a tiny portion of the universe.

For example, you might be pessimistic about your life. You might be convinced that this is the one and only interpretation of reality. That you are just stuck with the way things are.

But what if you are seeing things in the wrong way? Perhaps you are on the cusp of the greatest chapters of your life.

For instance, Oprah Winfrey was born into a poor Mississippi farming town, and she grew up amid abuse and neglect. From the outside, it appeared as if she was destined for failure and poverty.

However, Oprah saw the truth: that she had the power to dictate her own destiny. And she was right. Not even setbacks and rejections could stop her as she went on to build a multibillion-dollar empire.

People such as Oprah know the secret: that the way we see things is magical. If we see it properly, there are no such things as barriers or setbacks. They are only opportunities to shock the world with our achievements. Everything can change once we see things differently.

You also have the power to open your mind and see larger truths. You can connect the dots to realize greater patterns. You can see how those patterns point to a bright, shining future.

And when you do this—when you see beyond your present reality—you are far more likely to attract inflection points.

Fortunately, you have a guide who can help transform your vision. You can see her. She's waiting for you. She is your Positive Self.

Look up. There she stands, blazing with life. Her smile could light up galaxies. Those eyes? They've seen the future—your future.

Hear her as she says:

I am here to tell you a truth that will change your entire life. *The world isn't what you've been told it is. It's what you dare to imagine it could be.*

I stand before you not just as the president, but as you—a version of you who has walked the very path you're on now. And let me tell you something extraordinary: the distance between who you are today and who you dream of becoming isn't nearly as far as you imagine.

I remember those quiet moments of doubt. The nights when dreams felt too bold, too distant. I remember because I was you. But here's what I discovered—what I need you to understand deep in your soul: you have never truly failed. Not once. What others might call failures are actually the foundation of your destiny. Think about it. Every single time life knocked you down, you did something remarkable: you transformed pain into power. You alchemized tears into determination. When the world whispered, "Give up," you whispered back, "Watch me."

Do you want to know what I see when I look at you? I see someone who has been unknowingly practicing greatness all along. Those moments when you helped others despite your own struggles? That was leadership. Those times you kept going when everyone else would have understood if you'd stopped? That was presidential courage.

Your heart—that magnificent force that feels so deeply, cares so intensely—that's not your weakness. It's your superpower. Your sensitivity lets you understand others in ways that will transform lives. Your empathy will build bridges where others see only chasms.

Let me share a secret about destiny: it loves the audacious. It favors those who dare to be magnificently, unapologetically themselves. And you—yes, you—are sitting on a reservoir of untapped audacity that would take your breath away if you could see it.

Tomorrow is waiting for your voice. The future is hungry for your vision. Every obstacle you've overcome, every tear you've wiped away, every time you've lifted yourself up—these weren't tests. They were preparation. The universe wasn't challenging you; it was championing you, strengthening you, preparing you for the incredible journey ahead.

So here's my challenge to you: stop asking yourself if you're ready. Stop wondering if you're worthy. Instead, ask yourself: what if everything—every struggle, every setback, every moment of resilience—has been preparing you for something extraordinary?

Because I can see it so clearly: your future is a constellation of brilliant possibilities, sparkling with your courage, your compassion, your indomitable spirit. The world needs your unique light, your particular brand of magic, your special way of seeing and changing things.

Remember this moment. Let it sink into your bones. This is when you finally understand that you're not just capable of greatness—you're destined for it.

Now, take a deep breath. Feel that stirring in your soul? That's not just hope or possibility. That's your future calling. And oh, my friend, what a glorious future it is.

The time for doubt is over. The time for hesitation has passed. This is your moment to soar.

And I'll tell you this: from where I stand, the view of your future brings tears of joy to my eyes. Because I know, with every fiber of my being, that you are about to astonish yourself—and the whole world along with you.

Rise, my friend. Your time is now.

Part 2

Barriers to Inflection Points

SO FAR, YOU HAVE SEEN TEN OF YOUR ALTERNATE SELVES. TEN versions of yourself who reveal how your life could have gone. Ten versions who unveil your true potential.

If you encounter the right mentor, event, or words, your life could easily take such extraordinary turns. Because the multiverse is vast, wonderful and miraculous things regularly occur.

And they will occur to you as well. You will encounter many possible inflection points in your life. Moments in which everything can suddenly change, and your life becomes magical.

You just have to be ready for such amazing moments and opportunities.

To be ready, you have to completely open yourself to the universe. You have to be willing to consider new possibilities. You have to be open to new ways of seeing yourself and the world.

However, it can sometimes feel difficult to be so open to the universe when we cling to negative emotions such as apathy, fear, and impatience.

We worry if we aren't good enough. We fear our life will get worse. We grow increasingly impatient when we don't have the life we want right now.

When we are immersed in such negative states of mind, we become closed off. When we are unwilling to let go of our grievances, pain, and anxieties, we cannot access the opportunities the universe offers us.

But you are now ready to fight for your dreams.

You have seen the wonderful and empowering ways your life can go. You are determined to seize life's golden opportunities and overcome all the barriers that stand in your way.

You are ready for your new life to begin.

Over the next chapters, we will discuss eight of the principal barriers in your mind. Eight barriers that stop you from attracting inflection points and manifesting.

We will teach you how to overcome each one in an empowering way. By daring to confront these negative barriers in your mind, you send a clear signal to the universe. You declare that you are ready to embrace the next stage of your life.

You are willing to cast aside the past and start anew. You are ready to embark on a brand-new adventure. One that takes your breath away and makes you feel alive.

Chapter 11

Doubt

SOMETIMES WE FEEL DOUBT. A VOICE ARISES IN OUR MIND. IT tells us that we aren't good enough. That we will fail. That we don't have a chance. That we should give up.

This critical voice is overwhelming. It is always there. It is inescapable.

It seems to speak the truth.

But does it?

Here is the secret. A secret that all truly successful people know. The critical voice in our mind doesn't know anything.

Rather, it only speaks the words that society wants us to hear. This is why the critical voice always reminds us of our mistakes. It's why it constantly seeks to make us feel bad.

It is the voice of society itself.

And it continually seeks to put us in our place.

Never speak up. Never take chances. Never dare to question the status quo.

Be who society says you are. Know that others are better than you. Follow the rules.

Live in fear. Only think about the things that can go wrong. Know that failure is permanent.

This critical voice is why you have trouble manifesting your dreams. If you listen to it, you cannot envision new possibilities. Instead, you are stuck with the life society has given you.

So how can you begin defying society? How can you overcome your doubts?

You can do so by connecting with one of your alternate selves. A version of you who dares to question society.

Envision your Imaginative Self. See her laugh with joy as she stands before you.

Hear her speak:

That critical voice in your head? I know it well. I know how it whispers in the dark hours, how it tries to write smaller stories for your life.

But here's what that voice doesn't want you to realize: it's nothing more than an echo of old fears, a shadow puppet trying to pose as a giant.

Let me tell you what I see when I look at you. I see someone whose potential burns so bright it frightens that little critical voice. Of course it tries to dim your light. Your radiance threatens its very existence.

But here's the magnificent truth: you were never meant to stay small. You were born to illuminate worlds.

So let that critical voice speak if it must. Let it whisper its tired old stories. Because now you know the truth, you're not listening to that voice anymore. Instead, you're listening to the drumming of your own heart, the rushing of your own power, the clear, bright call of your own destiny.

So stand tall. Breathe deep. Feel the full weight of your power, the full reach of your potential. That critical voice is already fading, isn't it? Because finally, wonderfully, magnificently, you're listening to the only voice that ever truly mattered.

Your own.

Chapter 12

The Wrong Path

SOMETIMES WE GET THAT UNCOMFORTABLE FEELING OF UNCERtainty in the pit of our stomachs. We stare at our computer screen for hours, questioning our career choices. We lie awake at night, wondering if we've invested years of our life going down the wrong path. Every new relationship or project that once felt exciting now feels like a bad idea.

No matter what we do, we can't seem to quiet the questions that keep popping up in our minds.

Is this the right path?

Am I missing out on something even better?

Am I making a big mistake?

There is a persistent, ominous voice in our mind. It reminds us that we only have one life. That we can't waste our precious time and energy going down the wrong path. That we only have a few opportunities to get it right. That we might be permanently screwing up our life.

The voice grows louder with each passing day. It whispers doubts into every decision, turns excitement into anxiety, transforms hope into fear. It makes us second-guess even the choices that once felt completely right.

We find ourselves scrolling through social media, seeing other people's seemingly perfect paths, and the voice gets even louder: *See? Everyone else figured it out. Everyone else knows exactly where they're going.*

However, just like all the negative voices in our minds, this one is completely wrong. It overlooks one crucial truth: *you have a destiny.*

That negative voice doesn't understand the overall pattern of your life. It can't connect the dots to reveal larger truths. It doesn't see that you have always been headed toward something greater.

And here's what that negative voice doesn't know: getting lost isn't a detour from your journey—it's an essential part of it.

Think about every great adventure story you've ever loved. The hero never follows a straight line to their destiny. They wander through forests, get lost in storms, take wrong turns that lead to unexpected treasures. What seems like a mistake often becomes the very thing that transforms them.

Your life works the same way. Every time you feel lost, you're actually entering a space of infinite possibility within the multiverse. It's in these uncertain moments that life often hands you its most precious gifts—inflection points—if you're willing to receive them.

Consider this: what if feeling lost isn't a sign that you're going the wrong way but rather a sign that you're outgrowing your old map? What if this uncertainty is actually your internal compass calibrating itself to something larger than your current vision?

Being lost makes you look up and around. It makes you notice details you might have missed on a familiar path. It forces you to question your assumptions, to be creative, to reach out to others, to discover strengths you didn't know you had.

Some of the most successful and fulfilled people in history spent years feeling completely lost. They changed careers multiple times, lived in different cities, tried and failed at various ventures. But looking back, they could see how each apparent detour actually gave them exactly what they needed for their ultimate path.

Remember: you don't have to see the whole path to take the next step. You just need to stay open, stay curious, and trust that being lost isn't a problem to fix—it's an invitation to discover something new about yourself and your world.

To maintain your faith in your destiny, you can always turn to one of your alternate selves. Right now, visualize your Confident Self.

See her striding toward you. She is wearing a Valentino suit the color of midnight and heels that could pierce armor. Not a single hair escapes her dark French twist. Not a single doubt clouds her penetrating eyes. With every step, she proves that she is the very embodiment of confidence.

She stands before you for a moment as if she is assessing your true worth. Then she speaks:

> I need you to hear this—really hear this. You're not going through all this just to end up okay. You're going through all this to leave a legacy on the world.
>
> But I know it doesn't feel like that right now. I know you're scared. Your heart feels raw. Your dreams feel fragile, and the path ahead looks more like a maze than a runway. But honey, that maze? It is your runway.
>
> Own it. Because uncertainty isn't a weakness—it's your secret weapon. While everyone else is following their safe, pretty, predictable path, you're about to discover something magical.

Listen to me carefully. You're not behind. You're not doing it wrong. You're becoming. And becoming is a bold, messy, gorgeous process that looks like chaos until it looks like art.

The universe has big plans for you, sweetheart. Bigger than your doubts, bigger than your fears, bigger than anything you've dared to dream yet. But here's the thing about big plans: they need space to unfold. And that lost feeling? That's just the universe making space for magic.

Remember this: every single time you feel like you're falling behind, you're actually pulling ahead. Every time you feel like you're going the wrong way, you're actually creating a new way. A better way. Your way.

So here's what you're going to do. You're going to take all this uncertainty, all this fear, all this doubt, and you're going to wear it like a crown. Because that's what it is: proof that you're brave enough to become something extraordinary.

Trust me when I tell you the universe isn't testing you—it's betting on you. And so am I. Because I've seen what's coming, and it's more beautiful than anything you could have planned. All you have to do is stay open, stay fierce, and let the magic unfold.

You're not just going to make it—you're going to make it iconic.

As she finishes speaking, you feel it—that electric current of possibility running through your veins. Her certainty wraps around your shoulders like a designer cape, and suddenly your uncertainty doesn't feel like quicksand anymore—it feels like a stage, waiting for your next bold move. You realize that being lost isn't your weakness; it's your opening act. And the show? Grab your popcorn because it's going to be legendary.

Chapter 13

Insecurity

SOMETIMES WE THINK THAT WE AREN'T GOOD ENOUGH. We look at other people, and we see the talent, skills, and resources given to them. And we think, That is not us.

We find it impossible to believe in ourselves or our future. We think that we are too hopelessly behind everyone else.

As a result, every day is a challenge for us. Rather than happily marching toward our goals, we just try to endure life. We keep fixating on how we will never have a bright future.

In so many ways, this is a heartbreaking way to live. And this is the true tragedy: we don't have to do this.

You may believe that you aren't good enough. You may compare yourself to others and think that you fall short. But you would be wrong.

Because this is the truth: no one knows your true potential. No one knows your limits.

Society has told you that you aren't good enough, but it is a fact that every successful person was also told that they weren't good enough.

For example, if you look into the lives of famous artists, inventors, and leaders, all of them were initially told that they weren't talented enough. That they didn't have the "it" factor.

However, all of them did one courageous thing: they chose to defy society. They chose to not believe in society's words.

They chose to march to the beat of their own drum. To dare to achieve the things society told them they couldn't.

You can do the same. You can unlearn all the assumptions and expectations placed upon you.

For the first time in your life, you can see yourself for who you truly are.

You have something special to contribute to the world. The universe has placed you on this planet for a reason.

Fortunately, you have alternate selves who can help you reveal your true talents.

Visualize your Positive Self now. See her confidently stride to you. Observe the utter self-assurance in her eyes. Here is someone who dares to defy society. Someone who absolutely refuses to let society define her value or potential.

Hear her speak:

Let me tell you what I see when I look at you. I see someone on the edge of an extraordinary awakening. In the coming months and years, you will uncover strengths that will astonish you. You will find courage in places where you once felt only fear.

Your true calling awaits you, and it's far greater than the small dreams others have chosen for you. And when you find it, you will move through the world with such natural power that people will wonder how they ever doubted you.

Others may urge you to be realistic, to lower your expectations, to settle for less. But I have witnessed your future, and mediocrity is not in your stars. You will achieve things that will make your heart swell with pride and leave others in awe.

This isn't just hope or wishful thinking—this is the first chapter of your real story. Everything before was merely preparation.

The time has come to shed the heavy cloak of other people's expectations. Your soul is calling you toward greatness—the kind of greatness that makes your younger self feel seen and your future self feel unstoppable.

You are not broken. You are not behind. You are exactly where you need to be to begin the journey of becoming who you were always meant to be.

Chapter 14

Being Burned Out

SOMETIMES, WE CAN'T DO IT ANYMORE.

We are burned out, and we don't know how we can keep going. Society has demanded everything from us.

It has asked us to work until we are exhausted. Until we have nothing more to give. And then it has asked for more.

We don't know how long we can keep this up. No matter how hard we push ourselves, we have nothing left in the tank. We barely have enough energy to get out of bed.

We feel like hamsters furiously running on our hamster wheel. Getting nowhere. Giving everything we have just to stay in place. Too scared to stop.

We are in survival mode. We are just trying to survive this week. This day. This moment.

Deep down, you know that life shouldn't be like this. You shouldn't feel like a prisoner in your own life. But how do you escape?

You have been working so long and hard on a series of unfulfilling jobs and projects. You have given up countless hours of your life doing what society has asked of you. You have given up your autonomy. Your desires. Your needs.

You have tried to be okay with your life. You have tried to make peace with all your unrelenting demands and obligations. But it is hard to keep going. You feel as if you are trapped in a dark tunnel that leads nowhere.

Sometimes you wonder what the universe wants from you. What exactly it wants you to do. Whether this is how life will always be for you.

It is all too much to bear.

Yet there's an ancient truth that surfaces in moments like these: our greatest transformations often begin when we think we can't go on.

What you are going through right now is actually a sign from the universe. The universe is trying to tell you something.

The first thing you need to do is give yourself the luxury of time and space. Give yourself the opportunity to think deeply about your life. Let yourself feel the universe.

What is it trying to tell you?

It is telling you that you have suffered long enough. It is telling you that you are now ready for something new. That you are ready to completely change your life.

You being burned out is a sign from the universe that you are now ready for this monumental change.

But how can you do this? How can you leave your old life behind and start fresh?

Fortunately, you have a team of alternate selves waiting to help you. Showing you the many wonderful ways your life can go. Revealing your actual destiny to you.

To see some of the wonderful ways your life can go, try this visualization exercise.

Imagine stepping into a private viewing capsule at the Infinite

Realms Gallery, where your possible futures are waiting to be discovered.

The capsule, a masterpiece of design, seems to float on air.

"Welcome to your personal Journey of Possibilities," your guide says softly, her voice carrying an otherworldly wisdom. "Today, you'll witness the extraordinary paths that await you. Each story we'll see begins exactly where you are now—burned out and ready for transformation."

The capsule glides silently forward, passing through a shimmering veil of light emblazoned with "Your Destiny Awaits." The air itself seems to change as you enter what appears to be a vast dome of swirling light.

"We've arrived at the Revelation Chamber," your guide says, her voice full of reverence. "This is where visitors discover who they're truly meant to become."

Suddenly, you're surrounded by large screens, each showing rapid-fire visions of your future selves, each one more surprising and thrilling than the last. Your breath catches as you witness scene after scene of your own transformation.

On one screen, there is a version of you walking into your former boss's office—not with fear but with a powerful calm as you deliver your resignation letter. You're launching your own consulting firm, and his biggest clients are following you.

You almost gasp at this sight. Is that really you, standing so tall, speaking with such authority? You've spent years making yourself smaller, avoiding confrontation, carefully weighing every word. Yet here you are, radiating the kind of confidence you've only dreamed about. Your heart races with recognition and possibility.

The scene shifts, and suddenly you're commanding a boardroom of executives, your presence so magnetic that even the most skeptical investors are leaning forward, captivated by your pitch.

At first, you want to laugh. There must be some mistake. But then you catch the familiar way you tilt your head, the distinctive gesture you make with your hands. It is you, but a version of you that seems to have discovered some magnificent secret. This version of you isn't asking for permission to exist; she's claiming her space with an ease that takes your breath away.

Another scene materializes, and you're on stage at a TED Talk. Your future self shares your story with such raw authenticity that the audience rises in a standing ovation. Tears spring to your eyes as you watch thousands of people stand, moved by your words. All those thoughts and feelings you've kept inside, thinking they didn't matter—they're now touching lives and helping millions of people find their way.

The visions begin to accelerate, each one revealing another facet of your potential. You're a renowned art gallery owner in Paris. A sustainable fashion pioneer. A bestselling author. A venture capitalist funding other women's dreams. A sought-after executive coach. You feel your breath quicken as each new possibility unfolds.

With each new vision, your chest fills with an expanding sense of wonder. But it's not just the impressive titles or achievements that move you—it's the way these versions of you exist without apology or doubt. They radiate an unshakable energy that you recognize somehow, deep in your bones. Like a memory of someone you were always meant to be.

As you step out of the capsule, you carry with you the most profound understanding: these weren't just possibilities you witnessed—they were glimpses of your own potential, waiting to be unleashed. You finally realize that your burnout isn't a dead end. It's the universe's way of preparing you for your most extraordinary chapter.

Chapter 15

Impatience

SOMETIMES WE GET TIRED OF WAITING FOR RESULTS. WE MAY have been working on a project or goal for years, but we have yet to see the rewards we desire.

Or we may have been waiting for a long time for our lives to finally begin. We see other people achieve stellar results while we wait on the sidelines for our turn to shine. But our turn has yet to come, and we are starting to lose our patience.

We want results as soon as possible. We believe that we deserve better, and every day it hurts to endure our present circumstances.

We know that we should be patient. That we should follow in the footsteps of fabled inventors, who were happy tinkering in their garage, alone, without any concrete results for decades.

But we can't stand to wait one more day. We have been waiting our entire life for results, and we want to scream at the thought of waiting yet more months or years.

We can't do this anymore. And because of our impatience, it is hard to be at our best. We make it difficult to escape our circumstances.

Because of our impatience, we tend to rush things. We don't

spend enough time reflecting, thinking deeply, and being creative. Instead, we just keep grinding away, constantly repeating old ways of doing things.

We focus on being busy rather than being innovative. As a result, we never make real progress.

Thus, we remain trapped in a paradox. We would do anything to achieve concrete results. But this intense desire for change causes us to be impatient.

Because of our impatience, we sabotage all our efforts. This is why we may keep trying and quitting new endeavors. Because we think, *If it hasn't happened by now, will it ever happen?*

This is the negative cycle that countless people are trapped in. It defines their entire lives.

But there is a way out of this cycle of impatience. And the answer will surprise you. It is to do something that may feel trivial and unimportant. However, if you do this one action, it will literally change your entire life.

This is the action: laugh.

Laugh at the absurdity of life. Laugh at the silly challenges that life keeps sending you. Laugh at the nonsense of society.

Once you laugh, you make everything lighter. Then the present doesn't seem that bad. Then you don't feel impatient.

Such laughter is magical and transformative. It will have profound effects in your life.

It will even take away the dread you feel about work. Life becomes easier when you learn to laugh at the overbearing boss who takes himself too seriously. When you laugh at the silliness of worklife in our present society.

And of course if you take the world lightly, then the universe will send you things that are light and fun. It will be delighted by your humor and color your life in interesting ways.

Laughing at life will be difficult at first. It goes against decades of taking life too seriously. But you can do it. And once you do, life gets easier.

Imagine if you had spent the last ten years of your life living lightly. For those ten years, you laughed at setbacks. Every day, you appreciated the silliness and ridiculousness of normal life.

Had you lived in this manner, wouldn't your life have been better?

Without a doubt, you would have been more creative and daring. Setbacks and rejections would also have been easier to deal with. Everyday life would have been more fun as well.

Most importantly, laughter will inevitably attract inflection points. Moments in which you can suddenly and dramatically change your entire life.

It is not a surprise that those who can laugh at the world inevitably find success. They consistently attract the universe's attention and favor.

You can also learn this power. You can also learn to live lightly.

Thankfully, you have mentors throughout the multiverse. They can teach you how to laugh.

At this moment, visualize one of your alternate selves. Imagine one of your selves who fully embodies laughter. A version of you who understands that it is always possible to see the absurdity of life.

Specifically, imagine your Free-Spirited Self. See her now.

Picture her standing before you. She has your eyes, your face. But she has added touches. Glitter in her hair. Shimmering gold eyeshadow that catches the light with every blink. An outlandish outfit that is both beautiful and delightfully eccentric at the same time.

Most importantly, hear her laughter. It is your laughter yet somehow more musical and lighthearted. It fills you with joy.

Now, take an imaginative leap. Imagine seeing the world through her eyes. Imagine seeing life as a comedy rather than a drama.

See life through her eyes. Hear her gentle laughter at the silliness of the challenges that the world keeps sending you.

Listen to her giggle in amusement at the ridiculous people in your life. At everyone who takes themselves too seriously.

See her smile of anticipation every morning because she knows that funny and ridiculous things will occur that day.

If you consistently do this, if you regularly let yourself laugh at the world, you will definitely attract inflection points. You will attract special moments in which the universe sees and recognizes you.

Most of all, through living a more lighthearted life—in which you don't take setbacks too seriously—you will accelerate your rate of achieving your dreams.

Think about it: by incorporating more laughter in your life, waiting will feel easier. Even painless. Your typical morning frustrations will seem funny rather than annoying. That person who cut you off in traffic becomes a character in your daily comedy show rather than a source of stress. The coffee shop getting your order wrong becomes a silly plot twist in your morning story. That meeting that could have been an email? Now it's your daily dose of corporate theater, complete with the same predictable characters and catchphrases that make you smile instead of roll your eyes.

That time between now and your big break? It becomes your chance to observe all the absurd little moments life throws your way. That intimidating presentation? Just another opportunity to find humor in how seriously everyone takes themselves. Even those rejection letters can make you chuckle—after all, they're just proof that you're out there trying, living boldly while others play it safe.

When you learn to laugh at the small challenges, the big challenges naturally become lighter too. And suddenly, you'll find yourself moving toward your dreams with an ease you never thought possible.

Chapter 16

Lack of Motivation

SOMETIMES IT IS HARD TO FEEL MOTIVATED. ALL OF US FIND IT hard to feel inspired all the time.

There's a myth that we are supposed to be constantly motivated, that we are somehow broken if motivation isn't flowing freely through our veins every second of every day.

But here's the truth: there are days when we don't feel motivated. Even the most successful, unstoppable people on this planet have days when their usual fire is barely a flicker.

However, there is a specific method to spark your motivation and drive. By mastering the art of self-inspiration, you can create a relentless momentum that propels you forward, turning your boldest dreams into reality, one determined step at a time.

The key to reigniting your motivation is this: close your eyes, and envision that one magnificent dream—the goal that sets your soul on fire. Let your mind wander to the future that makes your pulse race and your spirit soar, the vision so powerful it lights up every cell in your body with electric anticipation.

If you have trouble visualizing your ideal future, try imagining this scenario: you wake in your multimillion-dollar beach estate, where modernist architecture meets coastal elegance. Floor-to-ceiling windows frame a pristine, private stretch of coastline, while Italian marble floors and soaring ceilings create an atmosphere of understated luxury. This isn't just your house—it's an architectural masterpiece featured in design magazines, yet it feels like home.

The scent wafting through your beach house is intoxicating—fresh coffee from your favorite local roaster mingling with sea salt and something sweet baking in the kitchen. Maybe it's those croissants your personal chef knows you love, or perhaps those famous homemade cinnamon rolls that have become your weekend tradition.

You reach for your phone, and there it is—a notification about your upcoming first-class flight to Bali next week. Just another adventure to add to your collection. Your banking app shows numbers that once seemed impossible—financial freedom that lets you choose how to spend each precious day. But it's not just about the money. It's about the life you've built.

Walking through your home, every wall tells a story. Here's you receiving that industry award in Tokyo. There's the photo of you swimming with whale sharks in the Philippines. The shelf holds souvenirs from your private villa stay in the Maldives, right next to the hand-carved statue from that little market in Marrakesh.

But what makes you proudest isn't the recognition. It's the profound impact you've had on others. Your inbox is filled with messages from people sharing how you've changed their lives. CEOs of Fortune 500 companies seek your counsel. Industry leaders quote your philosophies in their speeches. That innovative approach you developed has become a case study at top business schools.

Your schedule is full but not overwhelming because now you choose how to spend your time. Maybe today you'll take that important client call from your oceanfront terrace, then spend the afternoon working on your book while watching dolphins play in the distance. Or perhaps you'll fly to London tomorrow for that exciting new project, knowing your suite at the Ritz awaits. This isn't just success. It's freedom. Freedom to create, to inspire, to live every day exactly as you've always dreamed.

Now, as this vision fades back into the present moment, hold on to that feeling. That warmth in your chest, that flutter of excitement—that's not just a dream. That's your future calling to you. That's the life that's waiting for you, ready to transform from imagination into reality.

This visualization isn't meant to be a one-time exercise—it's a daily practice in possibility. Each morning, before the world's demands crowd your mind, give yourself permission to sink into these visions. Let them evolve and expand.

Today you might see yourself on that beach terrace; tomorrow, you might envision pioneering breakthrough technologies that change millions of lives or founding a revolutionary company that reshapes entire industries.

Don't limit yourself to just one version of success. The most powerful dreamers understand that infinite possibilities exist, each one as valid and achievable as the next. Remember this: across the vast expanse of the multiverse, countless alternate versions of *you* are living every dream you've ever imagined—even those you haven't dared to dream yet.

An alternate version of you stands on that Nobel Prize stage right now, accepting that award with tears of joy. Another version of you has already revolutionized space travel, making interplanetary exploration a reality. Yet another version of you has built that billion-dollar empire while still having plenty of time for family, adventure, and joy. These aren't hypotheticals. These alternate versions of you are out there, living these realities right now.

These aren't just philosophical musings. They are proof of what's possible. If these versions of you exist somewhere in the multiverse, then the potential for their achievement exists within you right now. Your task isn't to become someone else; it's simply to align yourself with these existing possibilities.

Every time you feel your motivation wavering, remember: you're not trying to accomplish the impossible. You're simply walking a path that another version of you has already blazed.

Your circumstances, your starting point, your past struggles—none of these define your future. They're simply the launching pad from which your dreams will take flight. The universe doesn't care where you started; it only cares where you're determined to go.

So close your eyes. Take a deep breath. And let yourself dream wildly, audaciously, without limits. Because somewhere across the infinite expanse of possibility, every dream you've ever had already exists. Now it's simply time to bring that reality to your life.

Your future is waiting. And it's even more magnificent than you've imagined.

Chapter 17

Beating Yourself Down

SOMETIMES WE SPIRAL. WE MIGHT HAVE MADE AN INNOCENT mistake or simply failed to anticipate the future.

Objectively, we were trying our best. We didn't know any better. Yet we can't forgive ourselves.

We start blaming ourselves for everything that has gone wrong, convinced that all failures trace back to us. We tell ourselves to shape up, to stop making such obvious mistakes.

Yet the missteps keep happening, sometimes the same ones over and over again.

In our minds, there is only one solution: we need to yell at ourselves. Beat ourselves down. Shame ourselves so we never make that mistake again.

We say things to ourselves that we would never dare say to another human being.

When will you learn your lesson?
What is wrong with you?
Why do you keep screwing up?

But no matter how much we criticize ourselves, the mistakes continue. We keep making our lives worse.

And we keep spiraling. We enter a dark place where joy becomes impossible to find. In this darkness, we can only see our flaws and mistakes. There is no hope. No possibility of redemption.

However, this isn't the truth. This is just a skewed perspective. The reality is that hope is not lost. You can still win.

In fact, there is a way out of this negative cycle. All you have to do is realize one important truth: *your mistakes don't matter.*

You think they matter. You believe that your mistakes are what prevent you from making progress. From reaching your dreams.

However, you are a human being. You are supposed to make mistakes. You are supposed to make bad decisions. You are supposed to do things that make you cringe.

This is the human condition for all of us. Even the best of us regularly make seemingly foolish decisions.

If you study the lives of great individuals, all of them made astonishingly bad choices. But despite these bad choices, they still achieved extraordinary things.

How were they able to do this? They knew one important secret: that mistakes happen to all of us. And because mistakes are unavoidable, they don't beat themselves down over them.

Think about all the time and energy you squander when you beat yourself down. All that time and energy could be spent building a life of success and happiness.

In other words, beating yourself down is the ultimate form of self-sabotage.

But you can stop this self-sabotage. It is possible to forgive yourself for being human. To laugh at bad decisions. To appreciate your great attributes even after a seemingly foolish mistake.

And when you stop beating yourself down, you invite inflection points. The universe will reward you for the grace and kindness you give to others—including yourself.

To help you see what life would be like for you if you gave yourself such grace, try this visualization exercise.

Picture your future self, but not just any future. This is you as the world's most fascinating enigma, a legend whispered about in boardrooms and penthouses across the globe. You're known by a title that makes everyone lean in when they hear it: the Phoenix. Why? Because you've mastered an almost supernatural ability to rise from any disaster, more powerful than before.

The story that cemented your legend still circulates in business schools and TED Talks. It was the day everything went wrong—your company's entire digital infrastructure crashed during the biggest product launch of the decade. Billions at stake. Careers on the line. The kind of catastrophe that would send most executives into a spiral of self-destruction.

But you? You walked into that crisis room like you were entering a party. Your energy changed the atmosphere instantly. There was something almost otherworldly about your calm. While others were drowning in panic, you were radiating an almost dangerous confidence. That was when everyone witnessed your superpower in action.

Instead of beating yourself down, you orchestrated the most spectacular corporate turnaround in business history. You didn't just fix the crisis—you transformed it into an opportunity so brilliant that *Harvard Business Review* devoted an entire issue to studying your strategy. The headline read: "The Billion-Dollar Mistake That Changed Business Forever."

Your influence is almost mythical. When you enter high-stakes negotiations, opponents who researched your every weakness find themselves disarmed by how openly you acknowledge and even celebrate your "flaws." Your famous line at the World

Economic Forum—"I don't avoid mistakes; I collect them like trophies"—sparked a global movement.

Your life becomes a master class in spectacular recoveries. That time you blanked during a keynote speech? You turned it into a moment of connection so powerful that people now pay premium tickets hoping you'll go "off-script." The day you wore mismatched shoes to a board meeting? It became your signature power move, spawning a fashion trend among young executives.

Your private life is equally iconic. Your penthouse is a testament to your philosophy. Where others display their successes, you proudly showcase your "beautiful disasters." That abstract painting in your living room? It started as a spilled wine glass that you let an artist transform into a masterpiece. Your most precious possession? A wall of letters from people who learned from you that their "rock bottom" was actually their launching pad.

In quiet moments, overlooking the city from your rooftop infinity pool, you smile thinking about your journey. You're not just successful; you're revolutionary. You've changed how the world views failure and success. Your legacy isn't about being undefeatable; it's about being undiminishable.

This isn't just a dream. This is who you become when you stop beating yourself down and start seeing yourself as the hero of your story. When you realize that your "mistakes" aren't your kryptonite; they're the source of your superpowers.

Because here's the truth: you weren't meant to be perfect. You were meant to be legendary. And legends aren't born from playing it safe. They're forged in the moments when you choose courage over criticism, advocacy over apology, rising over retreating.

This is your origin story. Your transformation from self-critic to superhero. And it all begins the moment you decide to stop being your own villain and start being your own phoenix instead.

Chapter 18

Fear

SOMETIMES WE ARE AFRAID, AND WE DON'T KNOW HOW TO STOP being afraid. The feeling follows us everywhere, like a shadow we can't outrun.

One scary thought can take over our whole mind. It grows like a storm cloud getting bigger. Day after day, it gets darker. We lie in bed thinking it will destroy everything we love.

Fear changes how we live each day. Our jaw stays tight until it hurts. Our stomach feels sick. We jump at every phone call. We flinch at every sudden noise. We can't remember how to take a deep breath anymore. At night, we play out our worst fears like a movie in our head. Even happy moments don't feel real. They just feel like a short break before something bad happens.

But here's the scariest part: sometimes we don't even know we're afraid.

You might think that's impossible. How could someone not know they're afraid? But it's like a fish in water. When fear is everywhere, you stop seeing it.

We make up good reasons for our fear. We say we're being "realistic" when we don't apply for better jobs. We tell ourselves we're "just being careful" as we check the locks five times. We say we're "not ready" for things we dream about. We keep our hopes small. We say, "Maybe someday," over and over. We think we're being wise, but we're really just hiding from pain.

Our shoulders stay tight all day, but we think that's normal. Our neck hurts every evening, but we blame our pillow. We wake up at three in the morning with our heart racing, but we say it's just the coffee. Our hands shake a little when we try new things, but we tell ourselves we're just tired. We feel a heavy weight in our chest before every meeting, every phone call, every decision, but we think that's just how life feels. We forget what it's like to breathe all the way down to our belly, to let our shoulders drop, to feel light.

Our world gets smaller every year. We stick to safe routines like they're walls that protect us. We say no to new things like they're threats. We avoid joy because disappointment feels worse. We don't see that we're trapped. We've made our cage look so nice that we think it's keeping us safe. But really, it's just keeping us small.

This is fear. And it rules the lives of countless people.

However, there is always something you can do. Even in the face of the worst, crushing, and unbearable fear, you always have a choice.

You can choose to question the stories your fear tells you.

You can notice how these stories always take place in an imagined future, one that hasn't happened and may never happen.

The truth is that your mind is like a dedicated but overzealous guardian, constantly scanning the horizon for threats. It creates elaborate scenarios of what might go wrong, believing that if it can imagine a disaster clearly enough, it can prevent it from happening. However, in the process of focusing on those imaginary scenarios, we worsen our lives.

For example, you might own a business, and you may be terrified that it will fail. You work day and night, micromanaging every detail, afraid to delegate even the smallest task. Your fear of failure drives you to hover over your employees, double-checking their work until they lose confidence and motivation. As a result, your business begins to fail. Not because of external factors but because your fear has created a self-fulfilling prophecy.

Or perhaps you're in a relationship, and you're terrified of being abandoned. You begin to overanalyze every text message, every slight change in tone, every delayed response. You ask for constant reassurance, need to know where your partner is at all times, become jealous of their other relationships. Gradually, your partner feels suffocated and begins to pull away. The distance between you grows—not because they wanted to leave but because your fear of abandonment built walls where there were none.

You can see the underlying pattern. Our fears lead us to act in counterproductive and sometimes self-destructive ways. By focusing so intently on imagined scenarios, we ignore our actual lives.

And remember that every single thought is a prayer to the universe. When we dwell in fear, we're essentially praying for more reasons to be afraid. This is why awakened beings know that mindset isn't just important—it's everything. Your thoughts today are creating your reality tomorrow.

In other words, you can fixate on a few unlikely, terrifying possibilities. And by focusing on them, you make them more real.

Or you can choose the alternative. You can open your eyes to larger truths. You live in the multiverse. In actuality, there are billions upon billions of possibilities open in front of you. And countless numbers of them are wonderful, surprising, and life-affirming. If you focus on these positive outcomes, then they will more likely come true.

At this point, you are probably thinking, *But how? How can I stop obsessing over my fears and focus instead on positive possibilities?*

You want to see past your fears. However, this may feel hard to do at first, for you have spent most of your life dwelling on your worst fears. It became a habit, a reflex that continually makes you feel scared and helpless.

Fortunately, you can break free of this cycle of fear. You can do so by connecting with your alternate selves. Those who have already conquered their fears. Those who have learned how to ignore the few horrible possibilities and instead focus on the countless dazzling possibilities in their lives. They are your guides and teachers.

At this moment, focus on one of your alternate selves. Specifically, visualize your Calm Self. See the utter assurance in her eyes. Note that she has your eyes but none of your fears or worries.

Now, this is the key action you can take. This is how you can take control of your life. *At this moment, take a bold, imaginative leap.*

For a moment, contemplate seeing the world the way your Calm Self sees it. Imagine how it feels to live with no fears. Imagine you live in a world where nothing bad can scare you or make you feel small. Picture yourself waking up every morning, ready and eager to explore the wonderful possibilities of life.

In this state of perfect fearlessness, anxiety no longer grips your chest. You get dressed while thinking about your goals, not your fears. You step outside your door feeling ready—not because everything will go perfectly but because you know you can handle whatever comes.

Notice how you move differently through the world. You no longer shrink yourself or hesitate before speaking. Your voice rises naturally, clear and strong, because you know your words have value. You share your ideas freely in meetings, start conversations with strangers, and pursue opportunities without second-guessing yourself.

Your energy begins to affect everyone around you in unexpected ways. People are drawn to your presence—this magnetic certainty that makes them feel anything is possible just by being near you. At dinner parties, you're the one everyone wants to talk to, not because you're the loudest but because your calm confidence makes others feel seen and heard.

You start to experience every part of life differently, like you've unlocked a secret level of living. That dream of starting your own business? You finally take the first step, knowing that even if you fail, you'll emerge stronger and wiser than before. That confrontation with a difficult family member? You handle it with such graceful honesty that it transforms your relationship.

Your fearlessness becomes your superpower—not because nothing scares you anymore but because you've discovered that fear is optional. You choose to focus on all the brilliant possibilities that could make your life extraordinary instead.

What you just experienced wasn't just a dream or wishful thinking. It was a glimpse of your true potential, a preview of the person you're meant to be. And here's what makes this moment so powerful: you created that feeling of fearlessness yourself. You proved that you already hold the key to seeing the world differently.

Let this truth sink in: fear is not your destiny. Every time you choose courage over comfort, possibility over doubt, you're reclaiming control of your story. Your negative thoughts may be loud, but your potential is louder.

Through practicing such exercises, you will become stronger and more confident. You will realize that your grand potential and countless possibilities of success in the multiverse will greatly outweigh any fear.

You can learn how to channel your alternate selves throughout your day. It will be difficult at first. You have been seeing the world a certain way for years. It is hard to break out of that habitual mindset.

But you can. And once you do, the entire multiverse will open before you. Through all the exercises in this book, you will practice channeling your alternate selves. You can do so even in the face of the most extreme negative thoughts and emotions. And then you will inevitably attract inflection points and manifest your greatest dreams.

Part 3

Your Unfulfilled Selves

YOU ARE PART OF A VAST SISTERHOOD. JUST AS THERE ARE infinite universes, there are infinite versions of you.

Each version of you encountered different life circumstances and events. Through quirks of chance and fate, some met the right mentor. Some were given the inspiring words they needed to do the extraordinary.

As a result, they led remarkable lives filled with meaning and purpose. They left behind dazzling legacies that inspired people throughout their worlds.

Others were not so lucky. They never encountered anyone who told them the words they needed to hear. No one told them that they lived in an infinite multiverse in which anything was possible. No one told them that they had the power to rise above their circumstances.

Consequently, these alternate selves never fulfilled their vast potential. They never chased their dreams. Instead, they just tried to survive each day, each moment. Frustration and fear ruled their lives. They always felt stuck, believing that it was impossible to improve their lives.

For a moment, let yourself feel the full range of compassion and empathy for these alternative selves. They could have done so much with their lives.

They could have traveled the world, immersing themselves in the beautiful and exotic. They could have dazzled millions with their breathtaking artistic creations. They could have been trend-setters who astonished millions with their audacity.

But they didn't. They have yet to truly live. They didn't know that they could be brave and strong. They didn't know they had what it took to be extraordinary. They never pursued their dreams with all their heart and commitment. As a result, they led quiet, suffocating lives.

Now, here is the question: what would you say to them?

You should always keep in mind that our lives can change at any moment. That even in our darkest hours, the sun can suddenly rise.

The same is true for these alternate selves. All it takes is the right word or message to inspire a different action or attitude. Such bold new directions inevitably attract inflection points—which will suddenly and dramatically change everything.

Over the coming chapters, you will learn about the lives of four of your struggling selves. After each chapter, you will be asked how you would inspire them.

This is an opportunity to teach others all the life-affirming ideas that are transforming you. That helped you understand you are a relentless creature without limits. That taught you to believe in yourself and in your dreams.

In the process, you will begin to comprehend these truths on a deeper level. You will better understand your own power and agency. You will spot new ways to attract inflection points, which will allow you to fulfill your greatest dreams.

Chapter 19

The Lost Self

YOU HAVE AN ALTERNATE SELF WHO FEELS DISAPPOINTED IN herself. Every day, she thinks about why she hasn't done anything great with her life yet.

She hasn't had head-turning looks. Or flashy accomplishments. She's never known what it feels like to impress anyone. Or feel wanted.

She is the type of girl no one ever notices in a crowd. And she knows it.

All she's ever done in life is work at meaningless office jobs. Where her clients yell at her and treat her like trash. Where her bosses never defend her and keep piling on the work.

Every minute of every day, she can feel her life slipping away.

She thought that, by now, at the age of thirty-two, she would have already figured out her life.

But as each day passes, she feels more and more lost. More and more confused. More and more angry that she didn't make the right decisions.

Worst of all, she can't seem to relate to her friends anymore.

The friends that are constantly moving forward in life. Getting promoted. Buying houses. Starting families.

She feels like that friend who is always in last place. The girl everyone feels sorry for. The person no one wants to be.

She desperately wants to restart her life. Fix her problems. Get a better job. Live a life that feels like it's hers.

But she feels so overwhelmed.

She doesn't know where to begin. She feels like she's too old to start over. That she's made too many mistakes that can't be undone.

Your alternate self feels stuck. How would you help her?

ANALYSIS OF THE LOST SELF

You understand the dilemma.

At thirty-two, she's caught in society's timeline of expected achievements—promotions, houses, families—while feeling like an outsider watching life happen to everyone else.

Her pain goes deeper than just career frustration. It's about invisibility—both in the workplace, where she's undervalued, and in life, where she feels overlooked.

Every client's harsh word, every friend's milestone announcement reinforces a story she's begun to tell herself: that she's somehow fallen irretrievably behind in life's race.

But the truth is that your alternate self isn't stuck. She is capable of suddenly and dramatically changing her life. All she has to do is start exploring different directions and opportunities. Such bold reinventions are inevitably rewarded by the universe.

The real challenge isn't her age or her past choices. It's that she's viewing her life through a lens of missed opportunities rather than seeing it as a continuous unfolding of possibilities.

She doesn't realize that every person who has ever achieved

something meaningful has first gone through a period of feeling lost, confused, and "behind." These feelings aren't roadblocks. They're often the very catalyst for transformation.

However, your other self has yet to realize these truths. She is locked into a viewpoint in which there is little hope. As a result, it is hard for her to muster the energy and self-belief to attempt new directions.

How would you inspire her? Before moving to the next page's speech, take time to craft your own words of wisdom. Consider what you would say to someone who needs to be reminded not just of their potential but of their inherent worth beyond any external achievements.

This exercise isn't just about offering comfort. It's about recognizing that within every story of feeling stuck lies the seed of transformation. As you write your speech, you can uncover universal truths about growth, resilience, and the courage it takes to begin again.

POSSIBLE ADVICE TO THE LOST SELF

Here is a possible speech you can give to your Lost Self:

> I know you. I know how drained you feel. You're sitting there right now, after another draining day at work, feeling the weight of every single no, every overlooked moment, every time you felt invisible.
>
> I know about the mirror you try to avoid, the social media you scroll through with an aching heart, the way you lie awake at night wondering where all the time has gone.
>
> At thirty-two, you feel like you're watching life happen to everyone else but you. Like you're stuck in the audience of a play where all

your friends are on stage, hitting their marks perfectly—promotions, houses, marriages, babies—while you're still trying to find your way to the theater door.

Let me tell you something about those meaningless office jobs, about the clients who yell and the bosses who pile on work like you're some kind of emotional pack mule: they don't get to define you. Yes, right now they pay your bills, but they are not your destiny. They are not your story. They are just a chapter, and you get to write the next one.

I know you look at yourself and see all the things you don't have. No long list of accomplishments. No purpose or passion to define your life. No indication that you are doing things the right way.

But you're looking through a warped lens, focusing on absence instead of presence. You know what I see? I see someone who has survived every single day of being underestimated and overlooked and still shows up. That's not weakness. That's warrior spirit.

You think thirty-two is too late? Let me share something with you. Vera Wang didn't design her first dress until she was forty. Julia Child didn't learn to cook until she was thirty-one. Grandma Moses started painting at seventy-six. And countless women completely reinvented their lives in their thirties, forties, fifties, and beyond. You're not too old—you're exactly old enough to know what you don't want anymore.

That overwhelming feeling? It's not a wall. It's a signal. Your soul is literally screaming for change, and that's actually a gift. Some people go their whole lives ignoring that scream, pretending it doesn't exist. But you? You're feeling it. You're awake to it. You're embracing it. And that's the first step to changing it.

Here's what I want you to do: stop looking at your friends' lives for a minute. Their timelines are not your timeline. Their paths are not your path. Instead, I want you to think about one small thing—just one—that would make tomorrow feel more like yours.

Maybe it's spending one hour researching a new career. Maybe it's taking one online class. Maybe it's updating your resume. Maybe it's just writing down what you actually want your life to look like without censoring yourself.

You're not starting from zero. You have something incredibly valuable: you know what you don't want. You know what doesn't work. That's not failure. That's market research for the next chapter in your life.

Those meaningless office jobs you've had? They've taught you resilience, professionalism, how to deal with difficult people, how to survive in less-than-ideal circumstances. These are not small skills. They're building blocks for whatever comes next.

And about feeling like the friend everyone feels sorry for—let me tell you something important: most people are too caught up in their own stories to be writing yours. And the ones who judge you? They're usually the ones most terrified of examining their own lives.

You're not too old to start over. You haven't made too many mistakes to turn things around. What you are is too valuable to keep living a life that feels like it belongs to someone else.

Start small. Start anywhere. But start. Take one tiny step toward the life you want. Then another. Then another. Don't worry about making up for lost time. Focus on making the most of the time you have now.

You're not the girl no one notices in a crowd. You're the woman who's about to show everyone, including herself, what resilience looks like in action. What transformation looks like in real time. What it means to stop waiting for permission to live the life you want.

Your story isn't over. It's not even stuck. It's just getting to the good part—the part where the overlooked girl realizes she's been a phoenix all along.

It's time to rise from the ashes.

Chapter 20

The Lonely Self

YOU HAVE AN ALTERNATE SELF WHO IS AFRAID TO TAKE ACTION. The thought of ruining her life with one wrong decision terrifies her. So she keeps waiting for the right moment before she makes a move.

It has to be the right job. The right guy to date. The right house to invest in. Everything has to be just right. Otherwise, she doesn't think it's worth having in her life.

But waiting this long has been very exhausting and frustrating.

She had hoped to marry her college sweetheart. She was sure he was the one. They went house hunting together. They even picked out names for their future children.

But he broke her heart. Out of nowhere. That blindside frightened her. It made her crawl into a hole where no one could ever hurt her again.

Suddenly, she found herself in a strange new world.

Trapped in a harsh, unforgiving reality where "happily ever after" didn't seem to exist.

She had always assumed that things were supposed to be easy, without any surprises or hardships.

But everyday felt so confusing and impossible. Overthinking

began to rule her life. The more she thought about any decision, the more she was convinced it was a bad idea.

This fear and dread ruled every part of her life, particularly her love life.

No matter how great a guy was, her mind picked at his flaws to give her an excuse to get out of the date. He was too short. Too talkative. Too nice.

Every guy just didn't measure up to what she wanted. To her, he was either too boring or too likely to break her heart.

So instead of going out on dates, she preferred to spend her Saturday evenings watching Korean dramas, where the male stars were always dreamy and never disappointed her.

She tried to stay in these fantasies because thinking about the real world, her real life, felt too painful.

But then, in a blink of an eye, ten years passed by.

Suddenly, all her best friends were getting married. They gleefully showed off their sparkly engagement rings. They constantly texted her photos of wedding dresses. And she tried to be happy for them. She really tried.

When she was asked to be the maid of honor at her best friend's wedding, she had to put on the acting performance of a lifetime. She had to pretend to be cheerful, to be the greatest cheerleader for her best friend, when she felt absolutely dejected about being single.

At the wedding, she tried to keep her cool. As she saw husbands and boyfriends sweetly bring champagne and macaroons to their significant others, she tried not to stare. As they playfully whispered inside jokes and gazed into each other's eyes, she tried not to yearn. Looking at those happy couples shattered her heart into a million pieces.

It made her realize that she would never have what they had. She would never know what it felt like to be cared for. To be cherished. To be wanted. To be loved.

She tried very hard to give up this fantasy of romantic love. She tried to embrace being single, knowing that many women don't need a man to be happy.

But she struggled so much. For every day was a reminder of all the things she didn't have. No one to hold her hand while walking on the pier. No one to go grocery shopping with. No one to hold her when she cried.

She could be alone for the rest of her life. And that thought made her feel hopeless. She felt utterly robbed of the future she could have had.

ANALYSIS OF THE LONELY SELF

Think about your alternate self—that version of you who feels like she is at a standstill. Who feels like there is nothing she can do but quietly accept her miserable fate.

The interesting thing is, she is not really trapped at all. She has the ability to make changes, try new directions, and reshape her life. Even a few steps in a new direction could dramatically change everything. It is always possible to attract inflection points.

The challenge isn't a lack of options; it's more about perspective. When we're in a difficult situation for a while, it becomes harder to see the alternatives that are actually available to us. It's like wearing the same pair of glasses for too long: we get so used to seeing things one way that we forget we can try on different lenses.

That's where you come in. Before looking at our proposed speech, take a moment to consider what you would say to this other version of yourself. What practical advice would you share? What small, courageous steps would you suggest? What opportunities might she be overlooking?

This isn't just about helping your other self; it's an exercise in recognizing possibilities. When we step back and think about how we'd advise someone else, we often tap into wisdom we didn't realize we had. Sometimes the best way to solve our own puzzles is to imagine solving them for someone else.

Take your time with this. Your insights might be exactly what's needed to help shift from feeling stuck to seeing possibilities.

POSSIBLE ADVICE TO THE LONELY SELF

Here is a possible speech you can give to your Lonely Self:

> Your true love is already out there, waiting to meet you, hoping you don't give up on them.
>
> And here's the wonderful truth: the moment you begin to truly live, you will find them. It's not a matter of if. It's simply when. Every step you take outside your comfort zone isn't just a maybe or a possibility; it's bringing you closer to an inevitable meeting that will transform everything.
>
> Those Korean dramas you watch? They're just pale previews of the real love story waiting in your future. The moment you step away from your screen and into the world, your own story will begin to unfold, and it will be more magical than anything you could have imagined.
>
> Real love, when it finally arrives, won't just be about grand gestures and perfect moments. It will be about morning coffee shared in comfortable silence, about someone who makes grocery shopping feel like an adventure, about hands that find yours exactly when you need them most.
>
> The years you've spent being careful haven't been wasted. They've been preparing you. They've been teaching you exactly what you

want, what you deserve, and how to recognize it when it appears. That college heartbreak? It wasn't an ending. It was your beginning. It was the first step on a path that leads directly to someone who will never dream of letting you go.

Here's what's absolutely certain: one day, you'll be walking down a street, or standing in line for coffee, or laughing at a friend's party, and you'll meet someone's eyes. In that moment, something will click into place. You'll feel it in your bones. This is different. This is real. This is what you've been waiting for. And you'll realize that every "wrong" turn, every delayed start, every moment of hesitation was perfectly timed, leading you exactly where you needed to be.

Your person is going to love every part of you, including your fears, your hesitations, and the time you spent hiding. They're going to understand why you waited, and they're going to make you realize why no one else was right before them. They're going to make every single day of waiting worth it.

So step out into the world. Say yes to that invitation. Smile at that stranger. Take that dance class. Join that group. Your love story isn't just possible—it's inevitable. It's already in motion. Every brave step you take isn't just a step into the unknown; it's a step toward someone who is also moving toward you.

Your happily ever after isn't just a fantasy. It's a guarantee waiting to be claimed. All you have to do is begin. Because the moment you do, the universe will conspire to make sure you find exactly who you're meant to find. And when you look back, you'll smile, knowing that every moment led you exactly where you were always meant to be: in the arms of someone who makes all the waiting fade away like a distant memory.

Chapter 21

The Pessimistic Self

YOU HAVE AN ALTERNATE SELF WHO CONSTANTLY LIVES IN FEAR that one day everyone will discover the truth about her. That she doesn't belong at her prestigious law firm. That she doesn't have the right education, right vocabulary, right charisma to fit into the upper echelon of society.

She always saw herself on the bottom of the totem pole. It was hard not to see herself this way, for everyone else in her law firm was a lawyer or on their way to becoming one.

And who was she? She was only a secretary. The only one who didn't go to college. The only one who felt lost any time someone talked about the stock market or global conflicts.

But she tried her best to hide her insecurities. She smiled and nodded and pretended to understand what was going on. She always tried her best to be sweet and agreeable. She always tried her best at everything.

No one could deny that she was a hard worker. She had no choice but to work hard, for in her world, money was hard to come by. Her dad was a gardener. And her mom sold roses by the freeway.

In her poor family, everyone was expected to work. Most of them dropped out of high school to do just that. And she was expected to do the same.

She was expected to give up her dreams of going to college. Stop fantasizing about what her life would be like if she could have that fancy law career. Because that kind of fantasy life looked easy and achievable on TV, but not in her real life.

Whenever she passed interns on their lunch breaks, she noticed that they were completely engrossed in their law school studies. They even seemed to enjoy studying, discussing interesting aspects of court cases, laughing as if they were in on some kind of joke no one else could understand.

She wished she could be like them. How they could stare at a page or breeze through a thick book and instantly know what it was all about. She never knew what it felt like to truly learn, as she was too busy taking care of her siblings in high school.

She felt like even more of an outsider during the annual company Christmas party. The cheery atmosphere and overly loud holiday music didn't put her in a festive mood. These parties felt like work to her. She had to have so many conversations and keep them going even though she had nothing interesting to say.

Sometimes, these conversations made her feel so uncomfortable, especially when coworkers asked about her future career plans. She never knew how to explain herself. For the truth was, she tried very hard not to think about the future. Ever since she was young, she had been in survival mode. She had never allowed herself to even think about career goals.

So throughout the party, while everyone else laughed and drank, she kept to herself. She focused on doing unimportant tasks, such as refilling napkins and cleaning tables. Anything to avoid awkward conversations.

Finally, as the night wound down, she only had one more

chore to do. Her boss asked her if she could upload the party photos to the company's social media page.

And just as she always did, she said yes. She stayed behind in the office while the rest of the staff merrily continued the party at the karaoke bar across the street.

As she went through each photo, looking for the best and brightest images, she was suddenly struck by something: *she wasn't in any of the photos.*

She was shocked and offended. Every other person in the office had at least one picture of themselves. Except for her.

She figured she wasn't looking hard enough. In a panicked frenzy, she spent an hour searching through the past ten years of Christmas photos, trying to find a photo of herself. And she couldn't find any. Not a single one.

For a long moment, she sat there, alone, in the middle of the dark and empty office, and for the first time, she understood her life.

She realized that she had never done anything special.

She had never graduated from college. She had never gotten that firm handshake for a job well done. She had never even gotten promoted.

She had never set goals for herself. Or even taken the time to think of them. She was so busy taking care of everyone else that she had never once thought about what she wanted.

Then, she got angry and started to regret every decision she made in life. Why didn't she dream about her own goals? Why wasn't she trying to make her life better? What was wrong with her?

She wished she had done her life differently. She should have stood up to her parents and gone to college. She should have sought help when she struggled in school. She should have thought about her future more instead of just enduring life.

But that is what she did. And now this was her life—the life that she was stuck with. There was nothing she could do. And that realization made her feel dead inside.

ANALYSIS OF THE PESSIMISTIC SELF

Before you offer guidance to your alternate self, recognize something extraordinary: she has already demonstrated remarkable capabilities that hint at her tremendous untapped potential. Think about it. She has successfully navigated a sophisticated professional environment at a prestigious law firm, adapting and learning every day, even without formal higher education. This reveals an intelligence and adaptability that many college graduates would envy.

Your alternate self stands at a powerful turning point. While she sees herself as "just a secretary," the truth is that she has been unconsciously preparing herself for a dramatic transformation. Every conversation about stocks she's listened to, every legal document she's handled, every professional interaction she's managed—these have been unofficial but have served as a valuable education. She has been absorbing the language, culture, and knowledge of a professional world that many never get to experience.

The path forward isn't just available—it's waiting for her. She may think that her life is over, but it is just about to begin. One word, one thought, one action can trigger an inflection point. She just has to see and recognize these life-changing opportunities.

On the next page, you'll find one possible way to speak to her. But first, we invite you to write your own message. Most importantly, help her see that her perceived disadvantages can become powerful advantages with a shift in perspective and the right support.

Take your time with this exercise. Your response may help unlock not just her potential but also your own understanding of how apparent obstacles can become steppingstones to an extraordinary transformation.

POSSIBLE ADVICE TO THE PESSIMISTIC SELF

Here is a possible speech you can give to your Pessimistic Self:

> Close your eyes for a moment and truly see yourself. You are the heartbeat of your law firm. When everyone else goes home, you're there, anticipating tomorrow's challenges, solving problems others don't even notice. This isn't just work—this is artistry. This is brilliance. This is what true leadership looks like.
>
> Your journey tells a story of strength, not lack. While others walked well-worn paths, you blazed your own trail. At an age when most were worrying about the prom, you were running a household. You've danced between cultures with grace, building bridges where others see walls. You transformed yourself into someone essential, someone irreplaceable. These are gifts born from your spirit.
>
> Think of your parents, tending those roses with calloused hands and unwavering hope. Each flower they sold was a seed planted for your future. You've already proven that you can transform challenge into triumph. Without a single formal lesson, you mastered the intricate dance of legal operations. Imagine the heights you'll reach when you spread your wings fully.
>
> In the next chapter of your story, you won't just be in the picture—you'll be its heart. Not because you learned to blend in but because you finally embraced what makes you shine: your journey from the

ground up, your ability to speak the languages of both struggle and success, your deep understanding of what it means to build dreams from dust.

Your tomorrow isn't about erasing yesterday. It's about seeing how each step, even the painful ones, shaped your path. Those nights helping your siblings study? You were learning to guide others. Those moments figuring out complex systems alone? You were teaching yourself to innovate. Every tear, every triumph, every moment of uncertainty has been sculpting you into someone extraordinary.

Soon, you'll walk these halls as more than someone who belongs. You'll be someone who helps others find their belonging. Your story will become a light for others who think their dreams are too big, too distant. This moment isn't your ceiling—it's your launching pad.

Your past isn't a weight holding you down. It's the wind beneath your wings. Every struggle, every sacrifice, every sleepless night has been preparing you for this metamorphosis. You're not just ready for more—you were born for more. And here's the beautiful truth: this is just the prelude to your symphony. Step into your power. Reach for the impossible. Trust that you are prepared. The world is waiting to witness the force of nature you truly are.

Chapter 22

The Numb Self

YOU HAVE AN ALTERNATE SELF WHO CAN'T REMEMBER THE LAST time she felt truly alive.

Her life has become this endless cycle of the same meaningless routine. Wake up. Drag herself to work. Come home too tired to live. Sleep. Repeat. Day after day after day until she can barely feel anything anymore.

Then one day, it hits her like a ton of bricks: she absolutely hates her life. Everything about it.

Here she is at a top financial firm in Manhattan—literally the exact job she spent her whole life working toward—and all it does is remind her every day how dead she feels inside.

No one warned her about this part. No one told her that after all those years of studying, all those sacrificed weekends, all that pressure to be perfect, she'd end up hating the very thing she killed herself trying to achieve.

Her chest tightens every morning as she walks into the office, knowing she'll spend yet another day staring at meaningless Excel sheets and helping rich, ungrateful clients make even more money. She can't even tell what day it is anymore. It's just an endless blur of meetings where nobody says anything real. It's where she has to pretend to care about decimal points and deadlines while feeling herself disappear a little more each day.

What terrifies her most is the crushing realization that this will be her life for the next thirty years—an endless loop of meaningless tasks. The thought of living this same soulless routine day after day, year after year, until retirement makes her physically ill.

Is this it? Is this the best her life will ever get? Is *this* the reward she worked so hard to achieve?

With all her will power, she tried to ignore these uncomfortable thoughts, placing them in the back of her mind. Pretending they didn't exist.

Until one day, her boss completely lost it during a morning meeting. In front of everyone, he brutally tore into her over a minor mistake, turning it into the most humiliating moment of her career. He went on and on, dissecting every flaw in her work, making sure everyone knew that hiring her was his biggest regret.

It was her worst nightmare come to life. The one thing that she had always feared was occurring right now in front of her. And in this terrible moment, when she was at the lowest point in her career, she suddenly realized something shocking: *she didn't care.*

She realized she hadn't cared for a long time.

Instead of going back to her desk to work, she decided to go outside for a long lunch. She had to gather her thoughts and figure out why she felt so numb.

As she walked downtown, she noticed it was alive with people actually living their lives—friends laughing over coffee, mothers playing with their children, couples holding hands. She stared at her untouched tuna Niçoise salad, the question burning in her throat: how did everyone else seem to know the secret to happiness? She had done everything right—followed every rule, checked every box—only to end up being the most miserable person she knew.

Feeling incredibly lost, she wandered around the block until she stumbled upon an antique store. When she went inside, she marveled at all the trinkets that had been collected from all over the world. But she was most drawn to a five-hundred-year-old relic from India.

It reminded her of when she dreamed of going to India as a child. That was the last time she had dreamed about anything. It was the last time she remembered feeling any joy or wonder in her life.

She wondered why.

When she returned to the office, she felt even more numb. She sleepwalked through the rest of the workday. She didn't seem to notice anything. Or care.

When her workday was finally over at eight that night, she gathered her things to go home. Then, she suddenly remembered she had promised to see her friend's play. She was honestly not in the mood to go. She just wanted to go home, take a shower, and lie in bed in the dark for a long time.

But she had promised her friend, so she went to the theater. It was a small one, only seating fifty people at most. She thought, *This is another meaningless play, put on by struggling actors and playwrights.* She just wanted it to be over.

Then, something happened.

Although she had seen her friend perform many times, this was the first time she actually noticed her.

She noticed how much fun her friend was having on stage. Her friend simply glowed. Through artfully donning pink wigs and glitter feather boas, her friend embraced joy and silliness on stage. She didn't care if she looked weird. She didn't care if she even stumbled on stage. And the fact that she was so carefree and surprising kept the audience roaring with laughter the entire night.

It was as if your alternate self saw life for the first time. And she felt it throughout her bones.

Until that moment, she thought her friend was delusional and living life completely wrong. She couldn't understand why her friend dropped out of college and waitressed at dingy restaurants. She used to think her friend was throwing her life away for a silly dream of acting.

But as she watched the audience around her laughing, she realized she had been the foolish one. Her friend was actually the wise one.

While her friend lived every day with purpose and a sense of adventure, she had lived life on autopilot, where every day felt scripted and predetermined.

She took life too seriously. She was afraid bad things would happen to her if she didn't have every part of her life planned out in the most practical way.

And because she had lived life too carefully, too fearfully, she now felt like a stranger in her own life. Stuck in the most lifeless life anyone could ever live.

As people trickled out of the theater, she sat there in her seat, quietly, numb to the life around her. She put her head in her hands, not knowing what to do with her life anymore.

ANALYSIS OF THE NUMB SELF

Your alternate self's story reveals something critical about success: sometimes our achievements can make us feel empty inside.

Your alternate self stands at a powerful turning point. What appears to be a story about hating a prestigious job is actually about something far more universal: the moment we realize we've built a life that looks perfect on paper but feels empty in reality. Her journey shows us that burnout isn't just about being tired; it's about living a life that's no longer aligned with who we really are.

Look closely at the story's key revelation. It wasn't the public humiliation from her boss that broke her. It was the surprising realization that she didn't care. This numbness wasn't a sign of failure. It was her soul's way of saying she was ready for something more authentic, more alive.

The contrast between her life and her friend's theater performance isn't just about different career choices. It's about different ways of living: one driven by fear and expectations, the other by joy and authenticity. Her friend wasn't happier because she chose acting. She was happier because she chose herself.

The path forward is both simpler and more profound than your alternate self realizes. Her current emptiness isn't a dead end. It's actually the beginning of her most authentic, most adventurous chapter. All those years of achieving and excelling haven't been wasted; they've been preparing her for something more meaningful than she's yet allowed herself to imagine.

Before moving to the next page and coming up with your advice for your alternate self, consider what her story awakens in you. Perhaps you recognize your own moments of wondering if there's more to life than checking society's boxes. Perhaps you wonder if you are doing all of this for *you* or for other people.

As you have learned throughout this book, every setback, challenge, or even tragedy is only the beginning to a better chapter in your life. Remember, within every story of burnout lies the beginning of a rebirth. A chance to create a life that makes us excited to wake up in the morning.

This isn't just about changing careers or making dramatic life changes. It's about remembering who we were before we learned to fear uncertainty more than emptiness. And that version of you? She's still there, ready for her comeback story.

POSSIBLE ADVICE TO THE NUMB SELF

Here is a possible speech you can give to your Numb Self:

> Listen to me because what I'm about to tell you is going to change everything.
>
> You know that numbness you're feeling? That emptiness that's making you dread every morning like it's a mandatory brunch with people you hate? Here's the truth that nobody's telling you: it's not a sign that you're broken. It's a sign that you're finally waking up.
>
> Let's get real for a second. You're not actually dead inside. You're just living someone else's version of success. And your soul is finally saying, "Yeah, no. I'm done pretending these spreadsheets are my passion."
>
> I mean, think about it. If you were really dead inside, would you have felt that spark watching your friend on stage? Would that Indian relic have touched something in your heart? No way. You're more alive than ever. You're just finally honest enough to admit that this perfect-looking life you've built is about as fulfilling as a LinkedIn humble brag.
>
> And can we talk about that friend of yours for a minute? The one waiting tables but lighting up the entire theater? She's not happier than you because she chose acting. She's happier because she had the guts to choose herself. That's it. That's the whole secret. While we're all out here trying to build the perfect resume, she's actually living.
>
> Here's what's actually happening: you've spent your entire life being the good girl, following all the rules, checking all the boxes. You were so busy building the life you thought you should want that you forgot

to ask yourself what you actually want. It's like you've been dating your job for years because it looks good on paper, but deep down you know there's no chemistry.

And you know what? That's okay. That's perfect, actually. Because you've already proven something incredible about yourself: you know how to achieve whatever you set your mind to. You've got the discipline, the smarts, and the drive. The only thing that needs to change is the direction you're pointing all that power.

Now, I know exactly what you're thinking right now. But what if I mess everything up? What if I make the wrong choice? Stop. Just stop right there. You want to know what's worse than making the wrong choice? Spending the next thirty years of your life dying a little bit every day in a job that feels like a never-ending Zoom call that could've been an email.

Here's what nobody tells you about these moments of total burnout: they're actually the universe's way of calling you higher. It's like you've been sitting in the waiting room of your own life, and the universe is finally saying, "Hey, remember when you used to dream about changing the world before you convinced yourself that a stable 401(k) was living your best life?"

You don't need to have it all figured out right now. You don't need a perfect plan. You just need to start listening to that voice inside you—the one that's been whispering about India, about adventure, about a life that actually means something to you.

Because here's the thing—and I need you to really hear this: you weren't born to be perfect. You weren't born to make everyone else comfortable. You weren't born to stare at Excel sheets until your soul leaves your body. You were born to be real. To be alive. To light up rooms with your authentic energy the way your friend does on stage.

So here's what we're going to do. Instead of seeing this burnout as your breaking point, we're going to see it for what it really is: your breaking-free point. Your life isn't over. It's finally about to begin.

Now get up. Get moving. Your real life is waiting for you, and it's got much better benefits than your current job—like wanting to be alive in the morning.

Conclusion

The Twenty-Week Manifestation Challenge

YOU ARE HERE FOR A REASON. EVERY DECISION YOU'VE EVER made, every turn and choice, every seemingly random event—all of it was leading you to this text, this moment, these words.

You are the reason for this book. You are the person who the universe needs right now.

You have read about the lives of several of your alternate selves. Through their examples, you can see your actual potential. What you can achieve with the right guidance and opportunity.

And because you have read and studied their lives, you can identify the hidden pattern. The subtle but unmistakable reason they could declare their wishes and have those wishes be seen and fulfilled by the universe.

For example, one of your other selves became an acclaimed artist in the mold of Frida Kahlo. To achieve this monumental feat, your other self did something that few people even attempt: she chose to be strong at every key juncture of her life.

Even when her art studio burned down, she chose to laugh

rather than cry. Without hesitation, she joyfully rebuilt her studio. She refused to dwell on negative emotions, such as regret and resentment. Instead, she consistently chose to dwell in a place of love, optimism, and gratitude.

This is the secret that your other selves discovered: *to be seen by the universe, you have to be an unexpected source of light.*

This is the certain way to attract inflection points, and this is your power. You have the ability to be a source of light no problem or setback can diminish. You can do something most people can't: you can see the light in the darkness.

Most people believe that the world is full of hardships. That the uncertainties and aggravations of the world are overwhelming.

But you are different. You were born to leave a legacy in this world. You have the courage to choose light over darkness. To choose love over fear.

This is the path your alternate selves walked. They chose love over fear, creation over destruction, and wonder over doubt. They were rewarded with an opportunity to manifest at extraordinarily high levels.

We all sense this truth: light attracts light. Love magnifies love. Hope kindles hope. These aren't merely poetic notions—they are the very physics of transformation. The universe responds not to what we do but to what we become.

You were given ten stories of your alternate selves, and they were chosen for a reason. They illustrate the Ten Laws that, if you devoutly follow them, will utterly transform your life.

These are the Ten Laws:

1. Thou shalt remember that victory will be thine.
2. Thou shalt live up to thy true strength.
3. Thou shalt see that doubts are always illusions.
4. Thou shalt strive for an unshakable calm.

5. Thou shalt choose to be confident.
6. Thou shalt let thy imagination run wild.
7. Thou shalt be free.
8. Thou shalt always remember that thou can be extraordinary.
9. Thou shalt embrace thy true beauty.
10. Thou shalt see beyond thy present reality.

By embracing these Ten Laws, you step into your power. You become not what the world expects but what your soul knows is possible.

Each time you follow these Laws, you become a source of light to the universe.

These Laws go directly against how many people are taught to live. Unfortunately, many have been taught to shrink from their light. To choose safety over possibility. Comfort over growth. When faced with failure, they retreat. When confronted with rejection, they diminish themselves. When challenged by discomfort, they seek escape.

They don't know that another way is possible. They believe that it is impossible to actually achieve transformation.

However, there is a way—a way born from ancient custom. From the mystical practices of Tibetan monks to the vision quests of Native American tribes, cultures throughout history have discovered that radical transformation can occur within a set number of weeks. A magic number that has long been part of human history.

According to ancient laws and traditions, twenty is that magic number. The number twenty is woven into the very fabric of transformation itself. The Mayans knew it. The Babylonians honored it. Nature herself works in cycles of twenty: wheat rising from seed to harvest, saplings becoming mighty oaks. Science now confirms what the ancients knew: twenty weeks marks the threshold where temporary changes become permanent transformations.

Your task is beautiful in its simplicity: for twenty weeks, embody the Ten Laws. Release what dims your light—the worries, the doubts, the fears. Embrace what makes you shine—kindness, patience, love. Your other selves have proven it's possible. Their power lives within you already.

Feel them now, these other versions of you, scattered across the multiverse like stars in the night sky. Feel their certainty in you, their unwavering faith in what you can become.

Mark your journey week by week. As twenty becomes nineteen, then eighteen, feel your power growing. By the final week, you will manifest with a clarity and force that once seemed impossible.

This is your Twenty-Week Manifestation Challenge. The path has been walked before—by you, in other lives, in other realities. Now it's your turn to shine.

Remember: your story matters. Not because of what you'll achieve but because of who you'll become. The universe has been waiting—not for your success but for your awakening.

Take a moment to reflect upon your life with all its twists and turns. Think about how often you wished for some way to turn the page, to seize the full measure of your vast potential—the potential you always knew existed within you.

All your directions and choices led you to this specific moment, to this book, and all the wisdom contained within it.

Such moments—when everything comes together—are exceedingly rare. It isn't often that a person encounters the exact means to reach their greatest wishes.

But this is what is happening to you. Everything is ready. Everything is in alignment.

All you have to do is follow the examples of your other selves. All you have to do is, for twenty weeks, embody the Ten Laws.

Many people live their entire lives without ever having the courage to stop and say, "Is this all there is?" They just keep moving, keep accepting, keep sleepwalking through their days.

But you've chosen differently. You've chosen to awaken. And that awakening—that uncomfortable, painful, beautiful awakening—is your doorway to transformation.

The universe has orchestrated every detail to bring you here. Every struggle that tested you, every triumph that lifted you, every disappointment that taught you—all of it was preparation for now.

Twenty weeks. Ten Laws. One extraordinary journey.

As you stand here at the threshold between who you've been and who you're destined to become, feel the energy of all your alternate selves surrounding you. They're not just stories anymore—they're proof of what's possible. Their strength flows through your veins. Their courage beats in your heart. Their wisdom whispers in your mind.

The universe is buzzing with excitement for what you're about to bring to the world. It's been saving a spotlight just for you, waiting for the moment you finally step into your power.

Your unique magic, your voice, your way of seeing the world—these aren't just gifts. They're essential pieces of humanity. And right now, in this exact moment, the world is ready for your magnificent story to begin.

Take a deep breath, and feel it: everything is aligning. Everything is possible. Your time has arrived.

This isn't just another ending. It's your beginning. The beginning of the most extraordinary chapter of your life. The chapter where you finally become who you were always meant to be.

Trust this moment. Trust your awakening. Trust the power that's rising within you.

www.ingramcontent.com/pod-product-compliance
Lightning Source LLC
Chambersburg PA
CBHW060524080526
44586CB00012B/605